Blessing the World

What Can Save Us Now

Rebecca Ann Parker

Robert Hardies, Editor

To Roger,

Blessings to you!

Reb

SKINNER HOUSE BOOKS
BOSTON

Copyright © 2006 by Rebecca Ann Parker. Introduction copyright © 2006 by Robert Hardies. All rights reserved. Published by Skinner House Books. Skinner House Books is an imprint of the Unitarian Universalist Association of Congregations, a liberal religious organization with more than 1,000 congregations in the U. S. and Canada. 25 Beacon St., Boston, MA 02108-2800.

Printed in the United States

Cover design by Robert Delboy
Cover art *A Season of Change II,* © 2003 Eleanor Rubin, http://ellyrubinjournal. typepad.com
Text design by Suzanne Morgan

ISBN 1-55896-515-7
978-1-55896-515-7

Library of Congress Cataloging-in-Publication Data

Parker, Rebecca Ann.
  Blessing the world : what can save us now / by Rebecca Ann Parker ;
Robert Hardies, editor.
      p. cm.
    ISBN-13: 978-1-55896-515-7 (pbk. : alk. paper)
    ISBN-10: 1-55896-515-7 (pbk. : alk. paper) 1.Violence--Religious
aspects—Unitarian Universalists. 2. Suffering—Religious
aspects—Unitarian Universalists. 3. Despair—Religious
aspects—Christianity. 4. Redemption—Unitarian Universalists. I.
Hardies, Robert. II. Title.

BX9841.3.P37 2006
261.8—dc22   2006010497

09 08 07
5 4 3 2

We gratefully acknowledge permission for the following materials:

Excerpt from "We Are Not Our Own" by Brian Wren, © 1989 Hope Publishing Co., Carol Stream, IL 60188. All rights reserved. Used by permission.

Excerpts adapted from *Proverbs of Ashes* by Rita Nakashima Brock and Rebecca Ann Parker. Copyright © 2001 by Rita Nakashima Brock and Rebecca Ann Parker. Reprinted by permission of Beacon Press, Boston.

Lines from "Transcendental Etude," from *The Dream of a Common Language: Poems 1974-1977* by Adrienne Rich. Copyright © 1978 by W. W. Norton & Company, Inc. Used by permission of the author and W. W. Norton & Company, Inc.

BLESSING THE WORLD

CONTENTS

BLESSING THE WORLD

INTRODUCTION

by Robert Hardies

THERE ARE TIMES IN OUR LIVES when it feels like things are falling apart. When loss strips our days of joy. When death robs us of someone we love, or violence shatters our sense of security. When war, genocide, and injustice lead us to the brink of despair.

This is a book for those times.

Anyone who has ever wondered "How will I make it through this? How can I repair what has been broken?" or "Where is the hope for our world?" will find a companion in Rebecca Parker. *Blessing the World* is filled with life-affirming answers to these questions, answers that light pathways through despair and point us toward hope. You won't find greeting-card sentiment or pat theological answers; what you will find are stories. Stories of people who have known despair and rediscovered joy. Stories of those who have taken serious measure of the world's injustice yet still found reason for hope, who have faced death and lived to tell about it. Parker's reflections are gleaned from a life that has known both violence and grace. Her theology, like any good theology, is life-tested.

A central premise of this book is that moments of despair can be opportunities for spiritual and theological breakthrough. According to Parker, when our current faith is inadequate to deliver us from—or even explain—our reality, we have three options: We can reject our faith, we can deny our experience, or we can become theologians, wrestling with tradition and experience until we discover a new, life-giving faith. Parker invites us to become theologians, and this collection of essays, adapted from sermons, speeches, and published works, bears eloquent witness to the creative potential of this choice. Her theology isn't merely an academic exercise but an endeavor through which human beings try to repair what is broken in our fragile lives and world. Seen this way, theology takes salvation not only as its subject but its task. The practice of theology is, itself, a salvific enterprise.

Parker's unrelenting search for the redemptive forces in life makes this volume an important and timely contribution to post–September 11 theological reflection. If there is one thing we should have learned in the years since that horrifying day, it is that violence cannot redeem what violence has broken. Yet as death tolls rise and terror strikes with increasing frequency, world leaders still cling with a blind faith to the myth of the redemptive power of violence. Whether it is terrorists who kill in the name of God or governments who wage war with the trappings of a crusade, the faith is the same: God will save the world through violence. Rebecca Parker's theological life's work—so eloquently on display in this volume—is to expose the lie that violence redeems and direct us toward the forces that do, in fact, save and repair broken life.

Blessing the World begins with "Finding Our Way," a series of essays that ask the reader to take seriously the extent of the suffering in our world. While many secular thinkers in the 1990s wrote of the late-twentieth-century triumph of American-style capitalism and freedom, Parker focused on the rampant oppression and devastation of the bloodiest century in recorded history. In these essays, she demands that we, too, notice and account for the suffering. Failure to do so represents, for her, one of our greatest sins.

In order to place the world's brokenness in its proper theological context, Parker asks us to make an imaginative theological shift. Many people of faith spent the last years of the twentieth century anticipating an imminent Apocalypse, whiling away their time until God's dramatic intervention cleansed this world of sin and ushered in the Kingdom. Tim LaHaye and Phillip Jenkins' best-selling *Left Behind* novels are the most popular manifestation of this pre-millennial hope. Parker turns this hope on its head, suggesting that it would be more accurate—and more helpful—to imagine that the Apocalypse has *already* happened, that we are living *in* the aftermath of Apocalypse, not waiting *for* it. Such an imaginative shift forces us to consider in a theological context the extent of the devastation wrought by the twentieth century:

> We are living in a postslavery, post-Holocaust, post-Vietnam, post-Hiroshima world. We are living in the aftermath of collective violence that has been severe, massive, and traumatic. The scars from slavery, genocide, and meaningless war mark our bodies. We are living in the midst of rain forest burning, the rapid death of species, the growing pollution of the air and water, and new mutations of racism and violence.

How much more destruction will it take, asks Parker, for us to admit that we are—in a very real sense—living in the midst of Apocalypse? It is not some future hour but now; it is "not somewhere else," she argues in this volume's third essay, "but here."

Parker's religious imagination not only foregrounds the apocalyptic scope of the suffering of the twentieth century, it helps identify the redemptive tasks that lie ahead of us. It does so first by ruling out violence as a means to redemption. Parker points out that violence has brought us to the brink of destruction; if violence got us into this mess, *more* violence won't deliver us.

Instead, Parker argues that the religious task after the Apocalypse is to sift through the rubble of our broken lives and world, searching for the beauty that remains, discovering the truths that are worth saving and salvaging the wisdom that can help us rebuild the world on a foundation of love and justice. We must become "appraisers of religious value," she says, discerning truths from lies. Our guides in this theological search and rescue mission, she suggests, should be those who have born the brunt of the violence of the twentieth century, for they already possess knowledge about how to survive violence and oppression—

knowledge that can help redeem our current crisis.

What Parker outlines in "Finding Our Way" is a theological task very different from that practiced by many theologians. Typically, the discipline of constructive theology seeks to build a systematic and philosophically coherent framework for understanding God, humanity, and redemption. It presumes an order and tidiness to the theological enterprise that Parker's post-Apocalyptic worldview does not. Parker uses the metaphor of a house to describe the theological enterprise. In traditional constructive theology, each part of the house—the roof, the door, the windows—represents a different belief or doctrine, but each part fits snugly and tightly together because of the coherent philosophical system that binds them. But we can imagine Parker's house built from recycled parts: thick beams that have survived a fire, floorboards recovered from an old home, an antique picture window that helps us see the world in a particular way. This house is made strong not by its snug fit and air-tight logic but because its structural members have withstood the test of time and living. In this sense, Parker's theology is reconstructive rather than constructive; it is literally a salvaged theology of salvation.

Throughout these first essays Parker turns upside down all of the religious myths of beginning and end, Creation and Apocalypse, Genesis and Revelation, the lush garden and the crumbling city—and asks us to re-imagine each of them. Perhaps the greatest imaginative leap of all is that she can envision an end to endings and an eternal presence of beginnings.

In "Reconstructing Our Faith," Parker helps us lay the theological foundations for a more peaceful and just world. Her theme is established in the first selection, "Cornerstones," written soon after September 11, 2001. This essay will transport every reader back to the shock and horror of that fateful date and to the religious question that occupied our thoughts: "What can save us now?" Parker weaves the nation's grief with one congregation's story of recovery from a devastating fire, affirming our human capacity to rebuild.

Other essays in "Reconstructing Our Faith" draw lessons from the lived experience of real people. We meet a shell-shocked war veteran whose sister nurtures him back to emotional health and a suicidal pastor who stumbles upon the strength to live in the unlikeliest of places. We explore the ancient forests of Parker's native Northwest for signs of grace, and learn about courage from a little congregation in Seattle that sets its mind on justice. Along the way, Parker conjures our religious ancestors to provide commentary and advice. Hosea Ballou testifies to a God who loves beyond our wildest imagination. William Ellery Channing makes the case for divine presence within every human being. Charlotte Perkins Gilman shows how it makes a difference when theology is written by women. The message here is that the resources for our own salvation are available to us. We can discover them in the stories of our lives and the histories of our religious traditions. We can learn them from our minds, our hearts, and our bodies. Theology isn't rocket science. If we pay attention, says Parker, we already know how to save ourselves.

Among the forces that she names as necessary for our redemption, Parker highlights the willingness to be present to and learn from our experiences of suffering, the vital role of both love and anger in the work of justice, the transformative potential of powerful communities, and the understanding of human beings as interconnected and as co-creators of redemption. In one of her most personally intimate essays, "On This Shining Night," Parker tells of her own discovery of a transpersonal grace that sustains and embraces us, even in the midst of suffering. Love is the theme that runs through these essays. By giving love specific form and content, Parker rescues it from shallow sentiment and restores it to its proper role as a saving religious discipline.

In each of the book's first two sections, Parker highlights a different facet of liberal theology. In the first section she operates out of its prophetic tradition, pointing out injustice and suffering and calling us to account for them. In the second section, she locates herself in liberalism's humanist tradition, affirming that human beings—in spite of sin—do bear the likeness of their Creator and possess capacities for their own salvation. Parker's uniting of liberalism's prophetic and humanist traditions is reminiscent of James Luther Adams. Adams helped navigate liberal theology through the horrors of the mid-twentieth century, when two world wars, two atomic bombs, and the Holocaust rocked liberals' faith in human potential for good. Adams concluded that liberal humanism, when severed from its prophetic roots, was inadequate to the challenge of evil. Adams and Parker, then, share a liberalism whose faith in humanity is tempered by the prophet's attention to evil, but not shattered so that it loses sight of the redemptive capacities of the human race.

By re-uniting its prophetic and humanist traditions, Adams and Parker have shaped a theological liberalism that is closer to the faith of its American founder, William Ellery Channing, who neither shied away from human sin nor relinquished his faith in our God-like potential. Channing wrote in his sermon "Likeness to God,"

> I do and I must reverence human nature. . . . I know its history. I shut my eyes on none of its weaknesses and crimes. . . . But injured, trampled on, and scorned as our nature is, I still turn to it with intense sympathy and strong hope. . . . I bless it for its kind affections, for its strong and tender love. I honor it for its struggles against oppression, for its growth and progress under the weight of so many chains and prejudices, for its achievements in science and art, and still more for its examples of heroic and saintly virtue. These are marks of a divine origin and the pledges of a celestial inheritance.

If liberals at the beginning of the twenty-first century can still join in Channing's stirring affirmation, it is because theologians like Rebecca Parker have healed the rift between liberalism's prophetic and humanist traditions, providing a theological foundation upon which liberals can act to bless the world.

In the final series of essays, "Blessing the World," Parker sends us out to do just that. Having located us in a time of great suffering and reminded us of the theological foundations on which a new creation must stand, she now sends us off to do the work of building that creation. Aware that this is no easy charge, Parker provisions us for the work ahead, suggesting spiritual disciplines and practices that will sustain us in our efforts to create justice.

Emerson and Whitehead are her guides here. Parker reinterprets Emerson's essay on "Self-Reliance" in the light of another of his lectures, "The Over-Soul," reminding us that the "self" that Emerson relied on was not an isolated, individual self but the indwelling presence of God in each and all. Such reliance doesn't isolate us; it unites us with others in the struggle for justice. We don't have to do this work alone. In the process theology of Alfred North Whitehead, Parker discovers for us another collaborator in the work of justice: God. In the book's last essay, Parker argues that one of the gifts of process theology is its unique view of God and humanity as partners in the work of redemption. Process theology conceives of a God who, in every moment, imagines the most just and beautiful outcome of that moment and lures and beckons us toward that outcome. Whitehead once called this alluring God "the poet of the world." Because God the poet relies on us to respond to this alluring call, human beings must make a choice. It is this choice that Parker confronts us with in a poem of her own at the end of this volume. She reminds us,

> Your gifts
> whatever you discover them to be
> can be used to bless or curse the world.

If God is, indeed, the world's poet, then Rebecca Parker is one of God's poets. After reading these essays I hope you will feel not only inspired to bless the world but blessed yourself for having spent some time in the presence of such thoughtful compassion.

FINDING OUR WAY

⚭

THROUGH THE RUBBLE

IMAGES OF ASHES LINGER FOR MANY OF US, even when our eyes are closed. For weeks after September 11, the smoke rose from the smoldering heap of collapsed concrete and steel at Ground Zero, where nearly three thousand human lives were turned to ashes in one horrible hour. More bombs followed. At a sidewalk café in Jerusalem. On a bus in Madrid. In the subways of London.

Similar images of rubble and smoke have greeted us in photographs from Afghanistan and Iraq, where war has killed thousands, destroyed great cities, and laid waste to the land. The toll of injured and dead Palestinians continues to rise as Israeli bombs and tanks raze cities and towns. A brutal genocide in Darfur, Sudan, has claimed the lives of thousands of adults and children. It's almost more than the heart and mind can hold. A friend recently said she felt like she was living with violence fatigue. I think that names it well for many of us.

And yet, this is hardly the first time we have been confronted with the human capacity for horrendous violence. Before the tragedies of the twenty-first century, many of us had already witnessed the violence of the twentieth: Rwanda and Guatemala, Auschwitz and Matthausen, Hiroshima and Nagasaki, the Gulag, Vietnam, Cambodia, Bosnia. The list goes on, and these are only the mass atrocities. There are also the individual and intimate experiences of violence that mark so many lives: rape, sexual abuse, domestic violence, and the cruel exclusions of heterosexism, ableism, and racism.

The list is mind numbing. How can we face it and understand our human capacity for such evil? How can we repair life in its aftermath and prevent its recurrence?

The Western Christian liturgical calendar has a season of ashes: Lent. It begins on Ash Wednesday, when believers receive marks of ash on their foreheads. During Lent, the faithful consider the meaning of Jesus' violent death and the obligation of people of faith to accompany those who mourn because of injustice and oppression. There is wisdom in this ancient Christian practice. Lent invites people to contemplate human vulnerability and lament the painful consequences of violence.

Theological reflection needs to begin here, with the reality that the lives of all of us are marked with ashes. It must confront the dual realities of our dependence on one another and our capacity for violence. We need our theology to be strong enough to assist us in facing evil. We need it to accompany us and guide us when violence breaks our hearts and severs the bonds on which life depends. We need it to help us find our way through long nights of pain when we have to discern how, in the aftermath of violence, life might be repaired, the perpetrators of violence stopped and held to account, and the escalating cycles of retaliation and revenge ended. We need our theology to speak to and from the experiences of the ashes.

Immediately following September 11, the Unitarian Universalist magazine, *UU World*, prepared a special issue focused on theology and evil. It probed the question of whether our liberal religious values are adequate for confronting evil. One of the people interviewed was Lois Fahs Timmins, the daughter of Sofia Lyon Fahs, the revered educator whose influence shaped liberal religious education for nearly fifty years. Timmins says of her experience in Unitarian Universalist religious education,

> We spent 95 percent of our time studying good people doing good things, and skipped very lightly over the bad

parts of humanity. . . . I was taught not to be judgmental, not to observe or report on the bad behavior of others. Consequently, because of my education, I grew up ignorant about bad human behavior, incompetent to observe it accurately, unskilled in how to respond to it, and ashamed of talking about evil.

Violence can do more than grieve our hearts. It can also shatter our faith, shake the ground of our beliefs, and reveal the cracks in our theology. What do we do when we discover that the religious beliefs we have placed our trust in are not adequate to address the violence and evil that confront us? What if we discover that our theology hinders rather than helps?

This is what happens to Job in the Bible.

Job is beset with heart-wrenching suffering and loss. Invading armies kill his people and his animals. Fire destroys his fields; a storm kills his children. His body is wasting away, covered with painful sores. Job's friends tell him it is God's punishment for his sins. But, they say, if Job repents of his sins, God will relieve his anguish and restore him to health and prosperity. Job recognizes that his friends are mouthing the standard theology of his religious community, but he doesn't like it. For one thing, he believes that God is just, and he knows that none of his sins merits this level of punishment. He refuses to accept a theology that says his suffering is God's doing. Job also knows the world. He sees that among the prosperous people in his community are those who have no reverence for God or Torah or who have gained their wealth by exploiting the poor. Yet, these blatant sinners are not punished by God. Job cannot accept his friends' pious certitude that God punishes the wicked and rewards the good. Their theology is not adequate for the realities of Job's life, nor does it address the violence and pain he experiences. Instead, it intensifies his pain by labeling him an outcast and making him an object of scorn. So Job argues fiercely with the theology of his day, saying to his friends, "You whitewash with lies. You speak deceptively about God. Your maxims are proverbs of ashes."

Rosemary Chinnici, retired professor of pastoral theology at the Starr King School for the Ministry in Berkeley, California, says that what happens to Job happens to most of us. We come to a time when we realize that the faith we have inherited is inadequate for what we are facing. Chinnici calls this religious impasse. I've learned from her that at such moments we have three choices: We can hold to our religious beliefs and deny our experience, we can hold to our experience and walk away from our religious tradition, or we can become theologians.

Chinnici recommends the third option, and so do I. Theological reflection becomes important precisely at times when human beings find themselves at an impasse between what they have inherited from tradition and what life throws at them. These are the moments when each of us has the opportunity to become a theologian—to take on the task, as Job does, of searching more deeply for truth, for a usable answer to the questions life asks of us.

Many Unitarian Universalists have learned this. Those not born and bred in the faith often come to Unitarian Universalism because we experienced a religious impasse. Secularism, or fundamentalism, or the religious tradition of our childhood was inadequate. We learned that we had to become seekers and take responsibility for forging the religious beliefs—the theology—that would be strong enough for life's challenges.

The state of our world now demands that we all become theologians. The violence of the twentieth and early twenty-first centuries requires that we reexamine fundamental religious questions: How do human beings survive violence and suffering? Can we be saved from that violence? When despair and anguish threaten to overwhelm us, how can we be restored to confidence? Can we rise from the ashes?

During the years I served as the minister of the Wallingford United Methodist Church in Seattle, I discovered that my theology was not adequate for the realities of violence and pain in the lives of the people I was called to serve. This discovery created a religious impasse for me, and I had to begin rethinking my theology. A story will illustrate.

One afternoon, a quiet knock on the church office door interrupted my reading. When I opened the door, a short, brown-faced woman stood on the threshold, bundled up against the chilly Seattle weather.

"Hello, pastor. I'm Lucia. I live down the block and walk by the church on my way to the bus." She gestured to indicate the direction. "I saw your name on the church sign. You are a woman priest. Maybe because you are a woman, you can understand my problem and help me."

"Of course, come in," I said.

She sat down and smiled, an expression both warm and sad. "I haven't talked to anyone about this for a while," she began, the smile fading and sadness deepening in her eyes. "But I'm worried for my kids now. The problem is my husband. He beats me sometimes. Mostly he is a good man, but sometimes he becomes very angry and he hits me. He knocks me down. One time, he broke my arm and I had to go to the hospital. But I didn't tell them how my arm got broken."

I nodded.

She took a deep breath and went on. "I went to my priest twenty years ago. I've been trying to follow his advice. The priest said I should rejoice in my sufferings because they bring me closer to Jesus. He said Jesus suffered because he loved us. He said, 'If you love Jesus, accept the beatings and bear them gladly, as Jesus bore the cross.' I've tried, but I'm not sure anymore. My husband is turning on the kids now. Tell me, is what the priest told me true?"

Lucia's eyes searched mine. I wanted to look away but couldn't. I wanted to speak, but my mouth wouldn't work. It felt stuffed with cotton. I couldn't get the words to form.

I was a liberal Christian. I didn't believe God demanded obedience or that Jesus' death on the cross brought about our salvation, but just that past Sunday I had preached a sermon on the willingness of love to suffer. I preached that Jesus' life revealed the nature of love and that love would save us. I said that love never breaks relationship, keeps ties of connection to others even when they hurt you, and places the needs of the other before concern for the self.

I could see in Lucia's eyes that she knew the answer to her question, just as I did. If I answered Lucia's question truthfully, I would have to rethink my theology. More than that, I would have to face choices I was making in my own life. After a long pause, I found my voice.

"It isn't true," I said to her. "God does not want you to accept being beaten by your husband. God wants you to have your life, not to give it up. God wants you to protect your life and your children's lives."

Lucia's eyes danced. "I knew I was right," she said, "but it helps to hear you say it. Now I know that I should do what I have been thinking about doing."

She planned to take courses at the community college until she had a marketable skill. Then she would get a job and move herself and her children to a new home. We stayed in touch as she took each step. Eventually, her husband sought help for himself. Lucia agreed to let him spend weekends with their children. "They got their father back," she said, "and I got my life back."

Almost everyone to whom I have ever told this story has been appalled at the theological counsel offered by Lucia's priest. We instinctively recoil from the thought that a religious authority would tell a human being to submit gladly to battering. It immediately strikes us as wrong. But the priest's counsel, sadly, was not unusual. Fortunately, because of the work of people like Marie Fortune and the Center for the Prevention of Sexual Abuse and Domestic Violence, most ministers and priests are now better trained to offer appropriate pastoral care to victims of family violence. Still, even the best pastoral care cannot always overcome the impact of a theological tradition that teaches that the highest form of love is the willingness to bear violence for the sake of a greater good.

From this moment of religious impasse, my pastoral experience led me to conclude that Christianity's traditional ways of speaking about the suffering of Jesus make it difficult for human beings to recognize their right to say no to violence. They make it difficult for us to understand love as something more than denying yourself for the sake of someone else. They also make it difficult for us to recognize violence for what it is, to see it operating in our world in systems that sacrifice human beings. And if we cannot see violence clearly, we will not contribute to ending it.

When religion says that Jesus was holy and good because in the Garden of Gethsemane he prayed, "Father let this cup pass from me, but not my will but thine be done," we tell victims of violence that they will be closer to God if they do not insist on their own will but submit to the will of an abuser.

When religion says that Jesus went like a lamb to the slaughter without raising his voice, we teach victims of violence that it is virtuous to remain silent in the presence of abuse. Many of the victims who have broken their silence about sexual abuse by Catholic clergy tell us that they kept silent for years because their faith had taught them that the priest was a representative of God. How can you accuse a priest of child abuse when God the Father required his own son to suffer humiliation and pain?

When religion says that it was the will of the Lord to bruise Jesus, we tell victims that God sanctions violence. Right after September 11, Rev. Jerry Falwell and others described the attacks as God's punishment on America. Falwell later apologized for saying that America's tolerance for the sins of feminists, liberals, and gay people led God to punish our nation, but he didn't retract his basic theological point: Violence is a punishment from God.

Too often, the dominant theology in our culture deepens the traumatic effects of violence instead of offering insight about how those effects can be healed. The effects of violence are complex, multifaceted, and often long term. In addition to harming the body, violence can overwhelm, numb, or fragment the human soul. Disassociation, nightmares, and flashbacks haunt the psyche of survivors. When a whole community experiences violence, it may develop an intense sense of unity as its members bond in grief and outrage ("United We Stand"). But this bonding is an effect of violence, and it is only sustained if the community remains in a state of terror, defining itself in vengeful bondage to the perpetrator. It does not translate into healthy, just community. Instead, human relationships break down, families come apart, and obligations of care are neglected. Resources that could be invested in health care, education, low-income housing, and services for abused children instead fuel huge increases in military spending.

Ever since September 11, I have wondered if we, as a nation, aren't resorting to an unexamined, inadequate idea about what will save us, an idea that has its roots in a theology of redemptive violence. We are all victims of a terrorist attack that has cost lives, disrupted our economy, and traumatized us. The paths by which we can repair the damage, heal the nation's wounds, call the perpetrators to justice, and contribute to the prospects of peace and safety for the world community are not easy to discern. As we feel our way forward, we must engage in significant reflection. It will not be enough to enact old scripts uncritically. Religious impasse doesn't just happen to individuals; it can happen to a whole culture.

The old script we need to examine is the one that says violence can save us. This theological idea is deeply embedded in our culture. In its internalized form, this theology says that self-sacrifice is redemptive. We are to bear pain in silence, absorb suffering and humiliation, or cut away part of ourselves, and trauma will be transformed. Life will go on. In its externalized form, this theology says that God redeems the world through violence as divine justice. Don't we, to some extent, reenact this theology when we adopt military strategies aimed at payback? Don't we act, then, on the belief that if we inflict humiliation, pain, and death on those who have harmed us, our trauma will be transformed and life will get better?

Is this belief true? Is the performance of this ritual adequate? It may be, and many people in the United States are counting on it. Harvard law professor Martha Minow notes the value of seeking retribution for harm. In *Between Vengeance and Forgiveness*, she says that though we often think of vengeance in a negative way, "it embodies important ingredients of moral response to wrongdoing," including notions of justice, reciprocity, and a sense of self-respect that demands redress. But, Minow continues, vengeance has its dangers:

> The danger is that precisely the same vengeful motive often leads people to exact more than necessary, to be maliciously spiteful or dangerously aggressive, or to become hateful themselves by committing the reciprocal act of violence. The core motive may be admirable but it carries with it potential insatiability.

Minow concludes by saying that revenge and retribution can often be self-defeating and illusory. She quotes psychologist Judith Herman: "People who actually commit acts of revenge, such as combat veterans who commit atrocities, do not succeed in getting rid of their posttraumatic symptoms; rather, they seem to suffer the most severe and intractable disturbances."

Since September 11, we have grappled with these questions. Initially, our public leaders projected an image of calm but firm resolve to punish those who harmed us without giving in to the desire for retaliation. Commentators urged us not to behave in ways that would escalate the cycle of violence and make us no better than the enemy we despise. By 2004, images from Abu Ghraib shattered our view of ourselves.

According to polls, around 90 percent of Americans originally felt we were right to bomb Afghanistan. Most Americans took pride in seeing the Afghan people freed from the repressive Taliban. But many were disquieted. We need to think more deeply about who is "good" and who is "bad." Doesn't the ritual of retaliation protect us from self-examination and allow us to hold onto a comforting picture of ourselves as innocent victims? Will the pain and humiliation of our enemy free us from the harm our enemy has caused us? Do acts of vengeance heal the nation's wounds and create a better future?

The theology that remains unexamined if we don't ask these questions has a long history. In the Christian West, the first holy war was launched in 1095 by a call from Pope Urban II. He promised the Christian knights he recruited that if they died their debts would be forgiven and their deaths would merit rewards for their families, just as Jesus' death on the cross merited the reward of God's mercy and forgiveness for all Christians.

According to Balderic of Dol, writing in the early twelfth century, Pope Urban II said, "Go and fight for the deliverance of the holy places . . . go and merit an eternal reward. If you triumph over your enemies, the kingdoms of the East will be your heritage; if you are conquered, you will have the glory of dying in the very same place as Jesus Christ and God will not forget that he shall have found you in his holy ranks."

Inspired by this promise, the crusaders mounted waves of violent attacks. They killed nearly one-third of the Jews in the Rhineland and then headed east to kill Muslims. The theology that celebrated Jesus' death as a redemptive sacrifice was the theology that justified the beginning of the Crusades. It is a theology that says violence is sanctioned by God as a means of driving back the infidel, restoring God's honor, and achieving payback for wrongs. The formal Christian doctrine of the atonement emerged during this time, published just three years later in 1098 by Anselm of Canterbury, Pope Urban's good friend.

The religious terrorists who flew planes into the World Trade Center operated with a similar theology. Holy warriors experience themselves as victims of an enemy's unjustified aggression and violence or feel threatened by an encroaching culture. Having been humiliated, they fight back in order to avenge injustices and restore honor for their people. They believe their own deaths will bring glory to their families, will be honored among their people, and will be pleasing to God.

We must grieve the history and present reality of violence

sanctioned by religion and advocate for a different vision of God. We must voice an alternative understanding of how life can be saved. We need to be saved from rather than through violence.

Throughout Christian history, many have argued against redemptive violence. In 1130, Peter Abelard countered Anselm, asking, "Who will forgive God the sin of killing his own child?" Though labeled a heretic, Abelard persisted in condemning the Crusades and advocated that Christians should respect Muslims and Jews. In 1805, writing in *A Treatise on Atonement*, American Universalist preacher Hosea Ballou said, "The belief that the great Jehovah was offended with his creatures to the degree that nothing but the death of Christ . . . could appease his anger is an idea that has done more injury to the Christian religion than the writings of all its opposers."

The Christian dissenters who shaped our liberal religious tradition advocated an alternative vision of salvation that directs us away from violence and toward actions of love and care for one another. They saw salvation in acts that honor the relational bonds of life and express awareness of the sacredness of all existence. They articulated an alternative to the idea that we are saved by Jesus' violent death on the cross. Rather, we are saved by following the commandment to love as Jesus loved. His loving life, not his violent death, becomes our example. Jesus is called Savior because he embodied and taught love.

Love speaks out in the face of injustice and oppression. Jesus confronted the religious and political leaders of his time who had co-opted the Jerusalem Temple and were using it to lay heavy burdens of taxation on the people in order to fund extravagant Roman building projects. We, too, need to raise our voices and call our leaders to account when their policies and practices harm people.

Love tends the wounds inflicted by injustice and sin and offers compassion in the presence of suffering. Jesus helped those injured in body and spirit. He healed the sick, fed the hungry, and comforted those who grieved. We are called to do likewise.

Love builds communities of inclusiveness and friendship that break the barriers of oppressive social norms. The community of friends that Jesus gathered around himself included people of all genders, rich and poor, outcasts and elite, rebels and conformists. Some of the early Christian communities that evolved in his memory expanded their inclusiveness to embrace Samaritans, Gentiles, and Jews, a multiplicity of ethnic groups, languages, and cultures. We, too, are to set a welcome table for all.

Love affirms the goodness of this world as God's dwelling place. It observes nature and reads the signs of God's providential care. It considers the lilies of the field and the birds of the air and concludes, as Jesus once did, that life is sustained and permeated by God's love for all creation. Therefore, love directs us toward creating abundant life here and now for all earth's creatures.

We know the manifestations of love: protest, compassion, generosity, community, inclusiveness, reverence. But theologies of redemptive violence too easily obscure the saving message of the world's deepest religious wisdom. We need to discover these themes afresh and come to know their meaning in the depths of our own experiences. We need to proclaim the message of love with our lives, embody these values in our religious communities, and actively work to create a society that rejects violence as the path to redemption.

Alfred North Whitehead observed that there are times when violence is a last resort in personal or national defense. He also reminded us that the most violence can do is to stop something, like a violent aggressor, but it can never create. It can never bring peace into being. It can never repair what has been lost.

Love is the active, creative force that repairs life's injuries and brings new possibilities into being. Love generates life, from the moment of conception to the moment when we remember with gratitude and tenderness those who have died. And in the darkest night, when our hearts are breaking, love embraces us even when we cannot embrace ourselves. Love saves us and redirects us toward generosity.

A theology adequate to the realities of violence in our world must speak from the depths of our life experience. It must speak words of anguish and words of hope. The anguish is this: Violence can break our hearts and efface the sacred goodness of life in this world. The hope is this: Love, in its myriad forms, can recall us to life.

Because such a gracious love surrounds us and offers us restoration, let us offer the world an unshakeable commitment to one another and to life. Let us refuse the path of violence and illuminate the path of peace. Let us struggle to address and redress the temptation to believe violence can save us, and let us place at the heart of our religious message a strong, creative, and transforming love.

∞

AFTER THE APOCALYPSE

ACCORDING TO POPULAR RELIGION, we are living on the eve of the Apocalypse. A catastrophic cosmic struggle is coming, when God's forces will battle the forces of evil. Evil empires will be destroyed, and from their collapse will rise a new heaven and a new earth. In place of the thousand years of wrong will come the thousand years of right.

Religious liberalism has its own variations on the apocalyptic dream. Our version doesn't imagine that old worlds are destroyed and new ones created simply by the act of a transcendent god. We put ourselves into the drama. We assign ourselves the task of dismantling evil empires, and we go to work hammering together the New Jerusalem. Think of the evil empires whose ruin we have tried to orchestrate: patriarchy, racism, homophobia, militarism, economic injustice, environmental abuse. And we know the new world we want to put in place. As the hymn "We'll Build a Land" says,

> We'll build a land where we bind up the broken,
> We'll build a land where the captives go free.

I am grateful for the energy, commitment, and service liberal faith inspires, but I have begun to believe that this theological worldview may no longer be adequate for our times. If we can imagine that the Apocalypse is not ahead of us but already behind us, consider how we might regard our religious task differently.

I live in an urban neighborhood in Oakland, California. Tracy, a twenty-year-old recovering crack addict, lives next door with her five-year-old son, Patrick. She often locks him out of the apartment, and I hear him outside crying, "Mommy! Mommy!" She yells back, "No! You can't come in!" Sometimes I talk to Tracy. Sometimes I silently pray for her and Patrick. And sometimes in the night, when the pitch of violent voices is high, I call the police.

My neighbor on the south side of the fence sends me hate mail. She writes that I am the worst neighbor she has ever had. She is a white kindergarten teacher, and she is enraged that I allow the black children from the apartment building to play in my yard. "Don't you know they are criminals?" She writes angry letters when she's intoxicated and later, when she sobers up, she pens sweet apologies. Her name is Mary, from the Hebrew, *mara*, "woman who has swallowed bitterness."

One Sunday afternoon, one of those children Mary fears is in my kitchen. Ronnie is seven and has come over to use my watercolors. He has been engrossed in painting for several hours. He gives me some of his pictures, choosing carefully which ones are for me. I tape them on the refrigerator and say, "Ronnie, you are really good at art!" Puzzled, he looks at me and asks, "What's art?" I get out some books about Picasso and Matisse, and I hold his pictures next to pages to show him. "This is art, and what you're doing is art. Some people spend their whole lives painting." His face is radiant with excitement. But society has already prepared a place for this child, and by the time he is twenty, his most likely prospects are jail, addiction, and death. Not long after that Sunday, Ronnie and his mom move away. Nobody stays in that apartment very long. I miss him.

One early morning last year, my Vietnamese neighbor responded to a knock at his door. The person at the door shot and killed him on the threshold, before entering the house to rob him of his modest possessions. Across the street from his house is a synagogue. This week is Purim, the Jewish holiday that commemorates the story of Esther, whose courage and guile saved her people when

Haman sold them for nothing into the hands of a king who would annihilate them. It is a season of grateful remembrance, but also grief. There were Esthers in Germany, but they did not prevail. The six million were not saved. Two years ago, this synagogue was vandalized during the High Holy Days. The front doors were marred by fire, and hate words were painted on the walls.

Around the corner, my Ethiopian neighbors are mourning. A member of their family was murdered in the crossfire of an argument outside a restaurant. The ritual mourning goes on for a month. I hear the sounds of women keening inside the house at a certain hour every morning. The men gather outside on the sidewalk, standing watch.

One Saturday morning, I walk down the hill to the Lake Merritt bird sanctuary. The sky is fresh and blue, and the sun is filling everything with light. People are out. Children and old folks are feeding the mallards, the grebes, the coots, and the Canada geese that cluster around. Lovers lie in the grass, inviting the world into their pleasure. The rippling waters of the lake reflect the rising, green hills; the white stucco church with its red tile roof; and the arbor that circles the edges of the lake, heavy with wisteria. I find myself struggling for breath. I've grown accustomed to violence and grief, but I cannot bear this beauty.

Another Saturday, I walk down to the lake to return a video at a store at the edge of the park. It's the weekend of the Festival of the Lake, and a carnival atmosphere is in the air. It has been a day of music, dancing, food, and thousands of people. Now curfew has begun, and people are supposed to go home. I walk among families climbing into their cars. Suddenly there is a charge in the air, like the feeling of dampness before a thunderstorm, and I hear the sound of breaking glass, a loud crack, and then another. I round the bend and see a crowd moving like an animal. Before I realize it, I am part of the crowd. Spread out across the wide boulevard is a slowly advancing brigade of police on motorcycles. They are riding hip to hip, their lights flashing red, their helmets heavy masks over their faces. Behind them a line of police cars moves at a funereal pace, sirens sounding a low growl. Voices on bullhorns are shouting instructions to us to disperse. I feel the need to run, to escape from this army of officers of the peace. The people around me are also frightened. A rock hits a streetlight, and glass splashes down into the street. I turn, move away, find my way home.

This is our world, filled with acts of violence, abuse, and racial hatred. Our response is grief, silence, distance, and paralysis—or sometimes gallows humor. When I arrive home from the brewing riot, I say to my housemate, "Sorry, we're having a riot. I couldn't get through the police line to the video store. We'll have to take the video back later."

"Okay," my friend says. "Do you think they'll waive the late fee?"

My hometown, Seattle, was required by the Reagan administration to implement emergency policies in case of a nuclear attack. One policy read, "In case of an evacuation due to a nuclear attack, citizens may ride the metro buses without exact change." This is our world.

We are living in a postslavery, post-Holocaust, post-Vietnam, post-Hiroshima world. We are living in the aftermath of collective violence that has been severe, massive, and traumatic. The scars from slavery, genocide, and meaningless war mark our bodies. We are living in the midst of rain forest burning, the rapid death of species, the growing pollution of the air and water, and new mutations of racism and violence.

At the same time that much is breaking down in our society, there are arenas of great vitality and freshness. The arts are flourishing. New movements in religion and spirituality are blossoming. Academic scholarship is bursting with contributions from people of color, diverse feminist voices, queer perspectives, postcolonial writers, and more. Computer technology, advancing at breathtaking speed and often characterized by a spirit of whimsy, is creating new patterns of human connection in cyberspace. Cross-cultural encounters and countercultural movements are opening up new possibilities in medicine, business, religion, and the arts.

Living in these times, I feel the simultaneous presence of violence, chaos, breakdown, loss, creativity, liberation, possibility, recovery, connection, and empowerment. While we are actively dismantling some things, we are bringing new things to life. Sometimes today's culture overwhelms me with a sense of tremendous speed and no brakes. "Stop the world! I want to get off," I feel like crying out. The desire to feel in control leads many to smaller and smaller spheres of activity. Tribal enclaves become increasingly attractive. Efforts to feel and see our time whole are overwhelming and intoxicating.

How do we live in this world? What is our religious task? The traditional response of religious liberalism is to place our hope in the future. Our apocalyptic myth imagines that the present world will come to an end and a new age will dawn. The liberal apocalyptic imagination skips the violent parts. It sees change coming through an evolutionary process—the gradual dismantling of evil empires and the eventual unfolding of life into greater forms of beauty and justice.

I have done my share of calling for the end of evil empires and announcing that the promised land is just around the corner, but I have come to believe that we need to let go of this religious myth. We need to face more honestly the conditions of devastation that we are in the midst of, here and now. As we enter the new millennium, we need to see ourselves as people living in the aftermath of cataclysmic violence rather than as people awaiting the overthrow of the present world order and the birth of the new. We must relinquish our innocence and see the world as it is, focusing our attention on the marks of past violence in our personal and collective experience. We must notice the breakdown, sorrow, and legacies of injustice that characterize our current world order. From this place of honesty, we must discover how we can live among the ruins.

In my dreams over the past twenty years, the recurring images of the world are postwar images: a city in smoking ruins at twilight, fire-bombed to ashes, and scavengers sifting through the ruins. The task is to walk among the ruins, find what can be saved, and gather up materials to rebuild. In the aftermath of Apocalypse, the religious enterprise can be imagined as a kind of salvage work, recognizing the resources that sustain and restore life—resources that are ready at hand, not in some distant promised land. After the Apocalypse, we accept our dependence on sources of life greater than ourselves and open our hearts to receive survival knowledge from those who have already found restoration. We know ourselves to be living in a time of breakdown and breakthrough, chaos and creativity, fragmentation and resourcefulness, pain and grace. Our tasks include tending to injury in ourselves and others, collecting resources buried in the rubble, and constructing shelters for body and spirit, family and community. Specifically, the religious task for those living in a postapocalyptic world is threefold.

Truth-telling. Through our preaching, speaking, and writing, the religious community must provide a clear-eyed description of the world. We must refuse to look away or distract ourselves with imagined future worlds. We must resist quick-fix sentiments, like "we are all one," when what we are actually doing is killing each other and tearing apart the interdependent web of all existence.

Salvaging. We must sift through the rubble and determine what needs to be saved. We must become good stewards of history and tradition, identifying vital resources contained in the wisdom of the world's religions and making them available to people who have lost them, including ourselves. In the mix of beauty and injustice that marks any religious tradition, we must judge what gives life and what oppresses. We must take our places as appraisers of religious values. We need the Sabbath candles, the house of study, the bread of communion, the silence of sitting, the teachings of Jesus, the dance of Sufis, the body-rhythm of gospel singing, the word of prayer, the narratives of the soul's dark night, the cross, and the ox-herding pictures.

We must resist stealing from one another and learn what gives us the right in any religious tradition to embrace its gifts. We must stop behaving like spiritual consumers who take for selfish reasons and give nothing back. We must see that the work of salvaging involves creating communities that shelter and protect religious tradition and, with generous hospitality, make these resources available to a world in ruins.

Choosing our guides. We must turn to those who have survived grief, victimization, denial, and paralysis. We must look to the witness of those who have found a way to live lives of dignity, honesty, creativity, and activism, and we must take counsel from survivors, resisters, and truth tellers. The guides we should heed are those whom William James called "twice born," people who have grappled with suffering, loss, and oppression and found a way to survive, such as African American women; lesbian, gay, bisexual, and transgender people; and those who have recovered from addiction.

A predominant sense of loss colors the tone of Adrienne Rich's poetry. Tragedy is the starting point in Alice Walker's novel *The Color Purple* and Toni Morrison's *Beloved*. These writers create in a context of grief and injustice. Their narratives speak of survival, restoration, and the attainment of peace. In a postapocalyptic world, we cannot locate hope in things not seen. We need tangible signs of survival beyond violence, just as the disciples of old did when they asked to touch the resurrected body of Christ. We will find evidence of resurrection in the lives of those who are present with us, bearing the scars of suffering and survival.

My friend Hadley Basque survived being a prisoner of war during the Korean War. He said that on long winter nights prisoners had to sleep in drafty barracks, with only thin blankets to cover them in the icy cold. The guards would light a fire and keep watch. Hadley could recognize the prisoners who had lost hope; they were the ones who slept by the fire. But in doing so, they lost their resistance to illness; they got sick and died. The ones who maintained hope never went to sleep by the fire. They survived.

In our time, hope means not running away from the icy, hard ground of suffering, violence, injustice, and deceit. It means savoring the sweetness of human love, lighting the Sabbath candles, smelling the spices, and opening our hearts to the sources of refreshment and grace that are given to us. Survival means reconstructing from the ruins a world of hospitality and peace. It means living as one of those who, as Adrienne Rich says, "with no extraordinary power, reconstitutes the world."

∞

Not Somewhere Else But Here

In 1976 I began a cross-country road trip with a friend on my way to seminary. We had time, so we decided to take back roads. One afternoon, the road passed through rural western Pennsylvania. Late in the day, we came down through hill country into a valley. It had been raining hard, and as we neared a small town, we noticed blinking yellow lights warning of danger. We saw fields covered in standing water and passed several side roads blocked off with signs saying *Road Closed*.

"Looks like they've had a flood here," we said. Coming into town, we crossed a bridge over a wide river. The water was high, muddy, flowing fast. Sandbags lined the roadway. "Gosh," we said, "they must have had quite a bit of high water to contend with here. Looks like it was a major flood!"

We headed out of town, following a winding country road, captivated by the evidence all around us that there had been a dramatic flood. Then we rounded a bend, and in front of us, a sheet of water covered the roadway. The water was rising fast, like a huge silver balloon being inflated before our eyes.

We started to turn the car around. The water was rising behind us as well. Suddenly we realized the flood hadn't happened yesterday or last week. It was happening here and now. Dry ground was disappearing fast. We hurriedly clambered out of the car and scrambled to higher ground. Soaked to the bone, we huddled under a fir tree. The cold water of the storm poured down on us, baptizing us into the present—a present from which we had been insulated by both our car and our misjudgments about the country we were traveling through.

This is what it is like to be white in America. It is to travel well ensconced in a secure vehicle, to see signs of what is happening in the world outside your compartment and not realize that these signs have any contemporary meaning. It is to misjudge your location and believe you are uninvolved and unaffected by what is happening in the world.

In *The Fire Next Time*, James Baldwin writes, "This is the crime of which I accuse my countrymen, and for which I and history will never forgive them, that they have destroyed and are destroying hundreds and thousands of lives, and do not know it, and do not want to know it."

I was born into the real world in a small town at the edge of the rain forest, on the coast of Washington State. The world was a mixture of violence and beauty, human goodness and human greed, tender relationships and exploitation, but I didn't learn to see life whole. Our town was the white settlement; upriver was the Quinault Indian reservation. The two communities were separated by a stretch of forest whose towering trees and thick undergrowth cloaked us from each other. Elton Bennet, an artist who lived in our town and went to our church, was one of a handful from our community who moved in both worlds. He had moved to Hoquiam in 1950 to make silk-screen pictures of the fog covering the trees, the clamdiggers in their red shirts on the shiny sand, the half-turned tugboats at low tide. His silk screens depicted the land and its diverse people. "They Speak by Silence," he titled one of his silk screens, in which a small band of Quinault moved along the shore between the forest and the ocean. As a small child, I watched Bennet pull the stiff paper from the inked cloth that created the image. It took the alchemy of art for me to learn that I had neighbors I did not know.

But in fact, the real world I was born into included richly diverse cultures and communities. In addition to the community I knew—the white settlement of people who logged the forests and fished the waters—there were other communities. The Quinault, Makah, and Puyallup Indians lived throughout southwestern Washington, preserving tribal ways against all odds. Chinese American cultural organizations in Seattle nurtured Chinese traditions and institutions at the heart of the city. Japanese Americans established temples and churches, landscaped gardens, shaped architectural styles, and farmed the land. Farm workers from Mexico harvested the apples in Yakima and Wenatchee and stayed to found Spanish-speaking towns. African Americans established churches, neighborhoods, clubs, and civic organizations.

By the time I came of age, neighborhood and church, economic patterns, cultural symbolism, theological doctrines, and public education had narrowed my awareness of the country I lived in to the point of ignorance. The Chinese, African, Latino/a, Japanese, and First Nations peoples had largely disappeared from my consciousness. Nor did I know the history of violence and exploitation that had occurred in my community. Two generations before I was born, Chinese workers on the Seattle waterfront went on strike for fairer wages, and the white majority beat back the strikers with sticks and guns. Just before I was born, the strawberry farms of Japanese Americans living on the Puget Sound islands were seized. Their land confiscated by the U. S. government, the Japanese Americans were uprooted from their homesteads and communities and taken away to live in concentration camps. In our town, the Ku Klux Klan and the John Birch Society supported overt white supremacist agendas. The Birch Society's large, bright highway billboard broadcasted hate. And the First Nations people went to court over and over again, seeking to secure the fishing rights and land sovereignty that were theirs.

I inhabited a white enclave that did not know and did not want to know the complex, multicultural history of the land in which we lived. The whitewashed world ignored the violence and exploitation in my country's history, as well as the resistance, creativity, and multiform beauty of my country's peoples. I was cut off from the reality of where I lived, whom I lived with, and what our history entailed of violence and of beauty.

There were moments of exception. My United Methodist congregation got involved in the Civil Rights struggle. From the pulpit, my preacher father exposed the redlining practices in our town. As a twelve-year-old, I went door-to-door with other members of my congregation, campaigning for open housing. Political involvement was exciting. I felt the importance of civic action.

But that same year, as I walked down the street holding hands with my best friend, Mary, we were passed by a car of hecklers who yelled profanities at us, words we didn't really know or understand. They turned the car around and drove by us again, calling us names, nearly hitting us as they sped by. Were they offended by the sight of a black girl and a white girl together? Were they enraged that we were holding hands, laughing and embracing one another, as we walked along the road? I defended my friendship with Mary and stood by my love for her when other students and teachers communicated that there was something wrong with us. But I learned that such love was dangerous. Love became intertwined with fear.

Probing the experience of being "cultured" into whiteness, Lillian Smith describes growing up white in the South as an education into fragmentation and denial.

> They who so gravely taught me to split my body from my mind and both from my "soul" taught me also to split my conscience from my acts and Christianity from southern tradition. . . . to believe in freedom, to glow when the word *democracy* was used, and to practice slavery from morning to night. I learned it the way all of my southern people learn it: by closing door after door until one's mind and heart and conscience are blocked off from each other and from reality.

Some learned to screen out all except the soft and the sooth-
ing; others denied even as they saw plainly, and heard.

The result of this closing-down process for whites, Smith
says, is that "we are blocked from sensible contact with the world
we live in."

Smith describes racism as a fragmentation of knowledge—a
splitting of mind, body, and soul; neighbor from neighbor; disciplines of knowledge from disciplines of knowledge; and religion
from politics. This fragmentation results in apathy, passivity, and
compliance.

When I speak of the ignorance created by my education into
whiteness, I am speaking of a loss of wholeness within myself and
a corresponding segregation of culture that debilitates life for all
of us. Who benefits from this alienation? Does anyone? What I
know is that I do not benefit from this loss of my senses, this
denial of what I have seen and felt, this cultural erasure of my
actual neighbors, this loss of my country. Thus educated, I
become less present to life, more cut off, and less creative and loving. Now that I recognize it, this loss disturbs me deeply. It is precisely this loss that makes me a suitable, passive participant in
social structures that I abhor.

Smith writes,

> Our big problem is not civil rights nor even a free Africa—
> urgent as these are—but how to make into a related whole
> the split pieces of the human experience, how to bridge
> mythic and rational mind, how to connect our childhood
> with the present and the past with the future, how to relate
> the differing realities of science and religion and politics and
> art to each other and to ourselves. Man is a broken creature,
> yes; it is his nature as a human being to be so; but it is also
> his nature to create relationships that can span the broken-
> ness. This is his first responsibility; when he fails, he is
> inevitably destroyed.

I want to inhabit my country, not live as if we did not belong to one another as surely as we belong to the land.

"Not somewhere else, but here" is a phrase from a love poem by Adrienne Rich that invokes love's imperative. The lover is drawn to what is present, to what is real. In its beauty and its tragedy, its burden of grief and its full measure of joy, life is loved through presence, not absence; through connection, not alienation.

In Pennsylvania, the moment my friend and I had to scramble to safety was a blessed moment—not because there is any virtue in danger but because it was a moment when consciousness was restored. We became present to our environment. We became more than passive observers. Our whole bodies, minds, and senses became involved with the requirements of the situation. We arrived. We entered. We left our compartment and inhabited the world. No longer tourists passing through the country, we became part of the place along with everyone else that day, in that corner of western Pennsylvania, in that storm.

I see this experience as a baptism because it was a conversion from distance to presence, from misconception to realization. It was an awakening to life, an advance into participation, and a birth into the world. This is the conversion that is needed for those of us who are white Americans. We need to move from a place of passive, misconstrued observation about our country to a place of active, alert participation. We need to recover our habitation and reconstruct our citizenship as surely, for example, as I and all women have had to learn to inhabit our own bodies and recover our agency when sexism has alienated us from ourselves. How do those of us who are white come to inhabit our own country? Here are four steps in the conversion.

Theological reflection. To earn our citizenship as Americans, whites need to deconstruct the effect on our self-understanding of theological imagery that sanctions innocence and ignorance as holy states. This theological imagery is strong. For centuries, Christian theologians have told the story this way: Adam and Eve in the Garden of Eden were innocent of themselves and of the knowledge of good and evil. Within the safe confines of the garden, all was provided for them. They were to ask no questions and be obedient to the rules outlined by God. In this state of primordial bliss, Adam and Eve were compliant and dependent. They cooperated with the divine ruler. This state was holy. The two were without sin, living in harmony with God.

This interpretation of the story sanctions innocence, ignorance, and lack of self-consciousness. It teaches that a carefully contained life, walled in by a providential God who is never to be questioned, is a good life. In the insular garden, human beings are in right relationship to God.

But temptation disrupted this primordial state of innocence. The serpent enticed Eve with the desire to taste the forbidden fruit and gain knowledge of good and evil. To gain knowledge, however, was to defy God—to go against the will of the divine provisioner. The consequence was a punishing exile. Adam and Eve were sent away from the garden, cast out from God's presence.

The implication is that to know the world in its goodness and its evil and to know ourselves capable of both is to lose God. To taste reality is to follow the devil. Such a theology is admirably suited to the preservation of compartmentalized, alienated states of mind. It blesses white privilege. It teaches those who have absorbed its message that goodness is aligned with innocence and ignorance. To not know the world is to know God. To know the world is to lose God. Furthermore, it teaches that a social structure in which one is abundantly provided for is not to be questioned. Abundant provision is a gift of God. This image comforts whites who thrive on current economic structures. It teaches us to accept privilege and never ask at what cost the walled-in garden is maintained.

As a white person, I have allowed this imagery to shape my self-understanding, even when I have consciously rejected the theology behind it. In practice, I discover myself to be deeply attached to being innocent and good. If I glimpse any blood on my hands, I will react defensively to preserve my identity and fend off the painful experience of shame that I associate with being exiled from the community I depend on for my survival and affirmation. Or I may attack myself, viciously trying to deny or destroy that in myself that does not conform to an image of innocent goodness.

The need to feel innocent preoccupies me and other whites. I strive to assure myself that I am blameless. If I am blamed or confronted with my complicity in violence, I become reactionary, for my sense of goodness has been constructed on the suppression and exile of my capacity to do harm, as well as on the suppression of offending feelings of love and connection that, I learned early on, don't belong in the garden.

At the same time, part of us never forgets that we have achieved our goodness at a violent price. We have a guilty conscience. At some level, we know that our pristine garden has been created by what has been exiled and exploited. This primordial violence lies beneath our sense of privilege and security. We fear exposure of our own deeper violence. We feel helpless in the face of it.

But theology assists us even here. The doctrine of the atonement valorizes violence as life-giving and redemptive. The interpretations of Jesus' death on the cross as a saving event speak of the violation that happened to Jesus as the will of God and the source of salvation. When this theological perspective prevails, either explicitly or buried within cultural patterns, the violence and abuse that human beings experience or perpetuate become valorized as necessary and good for the salvation of the world. Victims of racial injustice, identifying with Jesus, and perpetrators of racial injustice, identifying with God, may interpret their suffering as necessary, holy, and redemptive.

Most particularly, violating experiences that occur early in parent-child relationships can be misnamed as good. In *Learning to Be White*, Thandeka analyzes the violent shaming experiences that create white identity. Such shaming is theologically sanctioned as God's will. The suffering child is like the suffering Jesus, whose divinity is celebrated as his willingness to endure violation. The violating parent is doing what must be done as the divine enforcer of the orders of creation. The doctrine of the atonement reinforces violating and shaming experiences. Through these experiences, shamed children preserve their relationship to God and to goodness. I learn to interpret the violence that has formed my narrow, "white" identity as holy. If I begin to approach the underlying violence that creates white enclaves and white identity, the theology of my childhood tells me that violence is holy. Instead of facing my participation in violence, I can feel the pathos of violence with pious gratitude. Thus anesthetized, I will not seek to end it.

The sanctioning of violence as redemptive is at the center of William R. Jones's theological inquiry, *Is God a White Racist?* He shows definitively that no formulation of redemptive suffering can succeed at ending violence. Such a theology will serve again and again, in its diverse forms, to sustain structures rooted in violence.

To recover and become an inhabitant of our own lives and society, we need a different theology. A new theology must begin here, a theology that assists in an internal healing of the fragmented self, supports a new engagement with social realities, and sanctions a remedial education into the actual history and present realities of our country. Theology must direct us, like Eve, to taste the fruit of knowledge and gladly bear the cost of moving beyond the confines of the garden.

A different theology begins with the sanctification of knowledge and wisdom rather than the blessing of innocence and ignorance. The serpent can be reimagined as a representation of a God who calls us beyond the circumscribed comforts of the garden. To long to know, to reach for wisdom, to taste and see the bitterness as well as the sweetness, to come to know good and evil—these movements can be embraced as movements of God's leading. Leaving the garden, we leave the God who rules by reward and punishment, who offers security and comfort at the price of compliance to divine orders. We become sojourners in the world, accompanied by the divine serpent who moves in the earth, sheds old skins, grows new ones as needed, slumbers long, and wakes to strike quickly.

Remedial education. The journey to the realm beyond the garden begins with claiming forbidden knowledge. Because education cultivated in me and many others an ignorance rather than a knowledge of my country's history and people, I can begin to change things when I accept my power and responsibility to reeducate myself. Resources for such restored knowledge abound. Reading Howard Zinn's *A People's History of the United States* and Ronald Takaki's *A Different Mirror*, I become acquainted with my actual country. Immersing myself in the primary texts of First Nations' writers, Asian American writers, African American writers, Latino and Latina writers, and others, I begin to be aware of the world beyond my isolated enclave. Multiple voices surround me. I enter a miraculous Pentecost that has been sounding since before I was born. Takaki writes,

> Throughout our past of oppressions and struggles for equality, Americans of different races and ethnicities have been "singing with open mouths their strong melodious songs" in the textile mills of Lowell, the cotton fields of Mississippi, on the Indian reservations of South Dakota, the railroad tracks high in the Sierras of California, in the garment factories on the Lower East Side, the canefields of Hawaii, and a thousand other places across the country. Our denied history "bursts with telling." As we hear America singing, we find ourselves invited to bring our rich cultural diversity on deck, to accept ourselves. "Of every hue and cast am I," sang Whitman. "I resist anything better than my own diversity."

Knowledge is never an individual achievement alone. It is constructed by communities of people, and its construction transforms communities.

Ignorance is a precondition of violence. Once I, as a white person, have been cultivated into ignorance of my society—its multiple cultures, their diverse gifts, and the history of cultural conflict and exploitation based on racial categorizations—then I am easily passive in the face of racism's re-creation. But my ignorance is not mine alone; it is the ignorance of my cultural enclave.

Most of us do not know more than our community knows. Thus my search for remedial education, to come to know the larger reality of my country, is necessarily a struggle to transform my community's knowledge as well. As I gain more knowledge, I enter into a different community—a community of presence, awareness, responsibility, and consciousness.

I have learned that as a white American I must face the conflict that erupts between whites when fragmented knowledge begins to become whole again. This engagement among whites needs to take place with directness, wisdom, and a sustained commitment to build a new communion not dependent upon violence. It involves a spiritual practice of nonviolent resistance and nonavoidance of conflict.

Soul work. To sustain the journey beyond the garden, white people must turn inward as well as outward. We must form a new relational capacity, less hindered by the fragmentation and silences in our souls. We must find the path that takes us beyond the narcissistic need to have people of color approve of us or serve as our prophetic and moral compasses.

The construction of white identity involves the suppression of those parts of ourselves that we see as unacceptable and shameful, what many of us imagine as the "dark" part. This part of the self is the unjustly abused and despised aspect of the white person's own experience. Fragmenting our souls, we often suppress even our passionate feelings, sense of connection to others, ability to love, and ability to inhabit our own bodies. We then project onto people of color the lost part of ourselves: the silenced and abused "darkness" and the exiled and suppressed passion, emotion, and body. For whites, people of color come to represent the lost aspects of the self. Ambivalence and need characterize whites who feel better about themselves if they have intimate association with people of color, but such intimacy may lack the quality of an authentic relationship.

The inner journey for whites involves learning to withdraw our negative and positive projections from people of color. Whites must become relationally committed to meeting people of color as themselves, not as symbolic extensions of ourselves. To love more genuinely, whites need to recover and integrate the silenced, suppressed, and fragmented aspects of our own being. Others cannot do this work for us. We must extend internal hospitality to our whole selves, offer ourselves our own blessing, not seek it from those we use to symbolize our loss and shame.

Men who have projected onto women their own exiled capacity to feel need to recover the lost part of themselves rather than bond with women who will carry their emotional burdens for them. Likewise, whites need to accept the personal task of spiritual healing rather than project our own loss of humanity onto people of color, asking people of color to carry the burden of this loss. The soul work that whites need to do turns us to the sources of spiritual transformation that are transpersonal—to the presence of a deep reality of wholeness, connection, and grace that supports us beyond our brokenness and urges us toward a more daring communion.

Engaged presence. Racial injustice is perpetuated by whites who numbly disengage from the social realities of our time. Conversely, racial injustice will fail to thrive as more and more of us show up as present and engaged citizens.

Racism is a form of cultural and economic violence that isolates and fragments human beings. Engaged presence counters violence by resisting its primary effect. As a white person, the cure for my education into ignorance is remedial education. The cure for my fragmentation of self is hospitality to myself. The cure for my cultivation into passivity is renewed activism. Social activism becomes a spiritual practice by which I reclaim my humanity and refuse to accept my cultivation into numbness and disengagement.

The narcissistic preoccupation of whites in our present society is a symptom of how well established racism is. Hope lies in our ability to renew our citizenship through engaged action. Meaningful participation is advanced by specific concerns and sustained work. We do not have to take on the whole world at once. Racism takes specific forms in specific fields: education, health care, the justice system, economics, theology. Holistic engagement in any field offers significant opportunities to address and redress racism. As a theological educator, I take heart from what is accomplished when students do field work in the community, working on environmental racism, homelessness, HIV/AIDS, cultural survival, youth at risk, the prison-industrial complex, public education, or economic justice. In this engaged work, I see our white students move beyond the limits of their enculturation into ignorance and passivity.

Congregational life can provide a similar base community for the restoration of humanity. In my childhood, the church was the primary institutional setting in which racism was publicly named and its effects actively resisted. When church members took to the streets, we changed an unjust practice in our community. We also changed ourselves. Social action is an incarnational event. It mends the split of mind from body, individual from community, neighbor from neighbor.

A person of faith, seeking to inhabit his or her country out of love and desire for life, needs to be engaged in incarnational social action. Activism returns one to the actual world as a participatory citizen and an agent of history. Through activism, compliant absence is transformed into engaged presence.

The struggle for racial justice in America is a struggle to inhabit our own country, a struggle to become participants in its actual history and social reality. The struggle for racial justice is a struggle to overcome the numbness, alienation, splitting, and absence of consciousness that characterize the lives of white people and enable us to unwittingly replicate the life-destroying activities of our society, even against our will. It is a struggle to attain a different expression of human wholeness, one in which inner life is grounded in a restored communion with the transpersonal source of grace and wholeness and the primordial fact of the connectedness of all life.

The struggle is imperative. Racial injustice is not only a tragedy that happened yesterday, whose aftereffects can be safely viewed from behind the windows of one's high-powered vehicle; racial injustice is currently mutating and re-creating itself. Its dehumanizing effects are harming hundreds and thousands of lives.

In recent years, we in California have dismantled affirmative action; pulled the plug on public funding for bilingual education in Spanish and English in a state that is more than 50 percent Hispanic; and passed "three strikes" legislation that has dramatically increased the number of people in jail, a disproportionate number of whom are people of color. The construction of new prisons is a high-profit industry, and prisoners are being used for industrial labor at below-minimum wage. We passed a referendum to restrict immigrants' access to education and health services, and last spring we passed a referendum extending "three strikes" legislation to teenagers. A fourteen-year-old who steals a bike will already have a first strike against her. With this law in place, youth of color are highly at risk of becoming slave laborers in the prison-industrial complex. Meanwhile, public high schools in the Bay Area show a marked difference in the kind of education they offer. Schools with a majority of students of color provide few college preparatory classes, and only a small percentage of their graduates go to college. These statistics are reversed for the predominantly white high schools, where there are many college prep classes and a majority of graduates go on to college.

This is my country. Love calls me beyond denial and disassociation. It is not enough to think of racism as a problem of human relations, to be cured by me and others like me treating everyone fairly. Racism is more: It is a problem of segregated knowledge, mystification of facts, anesthetization of feeling, exploitation of people, and violence against the communion of our humanity.

My commitment to racial justice is both on behalf of the other—my neighbor, whose well-being I desire—and myself. I have been given the gift of life but I have not yet fully claimed it. I struggle neither as a benevolent act of social concern nor as a repentant act of shame and guilt, but as an act of passion for life, of insistence on life. I am fueled by both love for life and anger in the face of the violence that divides us from each other and from ourselves.

The habit of living somewhere else rather than here, in a constructed reality that minimizes my country's history of both violence and beauty and ignores the present facts, keeps me from effectively engaging in the actual world. I feel like a disembodied spectator as structures of racism are re-created before my eyes. But involvement in the steps of conversion—theological reflection, remedial education, soul work, and engaged presence— moves me from enclosure to openness. I step out of an insular shell and come into immediate contact with the full texture of our present reality. I feel the rain on my face and breathe the fresh air. I wade in the waters that spirit has troubled and stirred. The water drenching me baptizes me into a new life. I become a citizen not of somewhere else but of here. The struggle for racial justice in America calls all white people to make this journey. Our presence is needed; we have been absent too long.

∞

You Shall Be Like
a Watered Garden

IN FEBRUARY 2004, while the U. S. war against Iraq was in full swing and reports of lives lost came daily, an unexpected cloudburst of joy drenched the San Francisco Bay area where I live. Mayor Gavin Newsom announced that same-sex couples could legally marry. Overnight, beginning with Valentine's Day weekend, San Francisco's city hall became a sanctuary. With astonished grace, the hidden power of love revealed itself. From everywhere, pilgrims streamed to the newly born shrine. Couples who had been together for thirty and forty years legally sealed their commitment. New lovers made promises for a lifetime, dazed at the chance to make it legal. Wedding processions of every conceivable kind promenaded up the steps of the city hall—top hats and lace, leather and organic cotton, sequined gowns and T-shirts. They were accompanied by jazz, rock, African drums, classical string quartets, Chinese flutes, and even church choirs. The hullabaloo went on for weeks. Day after day, festivities multiplied, filling the streets with balloons, flowers, and dancing. Eros unveiled its presence in a myriad of bodies, cultures, colors, and ages. It was an epiphany of happiness, an outbreak of affirmation for the goodness of human sexuality, an unexpected, wildly welcome yes to the deep power of committed love.

Such a *yes* is not easy to come by. Conflict reigns over sexual intimacy outside the norms of heterosexual, patriarchal marriage.

Over the past thirty years, every major North American Christian denomination has been a battleground over the bodies and souls of lesbian, gay, bisexual, and transgender people. The struggle continues. Sometimes used as pawns in political battles that are predominantly about power and control, people's lives have been fractured by hostility and exclusion. Suicide has taken dear ones for whom locked closets have become prisons of despair. Hate crimes have killed gay people just for existing and showing their faces. Right-wing political strategists have used "defense of marriage" initiatives to bring people to the polls who will vote for conservative agendas and candidates.

When I first began working on BGLT (bisexual, gay, lesbian, transgender) rights in the early eighties, I tried to understand the religious heat in opposition to same-sex love. Why were some Christians so vehemently opposed to BGLT modes of loving? When a proposed law to curtail civil rights for homosexual people was on the agenda of our county council, church members and I went to the public hearings and testified against it. Based on our understanding of the teachings of Jesus, we advocated for BGLT people. But during two days of hearings, almost all the speeches were against BGLT civil rights. In the name of their Christianity, people said "gays" should be quarantined, locked up, exterminated, or at the very least, excluded from housing and health care.

Initially, I thought the opposition to BGLT rights was due to people taking Biblical injunctions such as Leviticus 18:22 legalistically and literally. But it is more than that. Christian conflicts about sexuality and gender are rooted in long-standing interpretations of the creation and fall stories in Genesis 1 and 2. Even when the Garden of Eden story is understood as myth or metaphor, it has been interpreted as expressing a theological truth: Sexual desire is the surest sin of humanity's sinful nature, leading humanity to rebel against God's sovereign rule and bring disorder into society. In *The City of God*, Augustine writes,

The undeniable truth is that a man by his very nature is ashamed of sexual lust. And he is rightly ashamed because there is here involved an inward rebellion which is standing proof of the penalty which man is paying for his original rebellion against God. For lust is a usurper, defying the power of the will and playing the tyrant with man's sexual organs.

The disobedience school of Christian thought regards Adam and Eve's original sin as their failure to do what they were told. In the garden, God commanded them not to eat some of the fruits. They disobeyed. In punishment, God exiled them from the garden and sentenced them to death. To rescue humanity from its exile and punishment, God sent Jesus to die on the cross. Divine justice was satisfied by Jesus' perfect willingness to follow God's command, to do what his "father" said—even when his "father" demanded his death.

Augustine's view of sexual desire as an expression of human rebelliousness has survived into the twentieth century in both theology and psychology. Freud said the sex drive must be controlled or culture would fall apart. Dietrich Bonhoeffer, for all his courage in the face of Nazism, followed the Augustinian view, writing in *Creation and Fall*,

> Sexuality is the passionate hatred of every limit, it is arbitrariness to the highest degree, it is self-will, it is avid, impotent will for unity in a divided world.... Sexuality desires the destruction of the other person as creature . . . violates him as well as his limit, hates grace.... Unrestrained sexuality, like uncreative sexuality, is therefore destruction par excellence.

Though there are Christian theologians who have viewed sexuality more positively, much Christian writing still implies that sexuality is dangerous unless it is controlled within well-defined boundaries. According to nearly all denominational pronouncements, only in heterosexual marriage can sexual intimacy be deemed moral and good. The church-sanctioned rejection of same-sex intimacy expresses fear that sexuality is dangerous. Boundless passion for boundless intimacy and joy is equated with defection from God's loving rule. Same-sex love is a radically out-of-bounds form of sexual expression. It is apostasy—the unforgivable sin.

Hidden within this suspicion of sexuality lies the view that the ideal relation to God resembles a monogamous, heterosexual marriage in which the male is superior and the female inferior. In this binary construction of gender, regarded as ordained by God at creation, the soul plays the part of the wife and is stereotypically female: passive, empty, dependent, and above all, obedient. God plays the part of the husband and is stereotypically male: authoritative, active, providential, and above all, commanding. The soul depends on God for meaning, direction, and survival. Any intimacy outside this holy bond transgresses right relationship with a jealous God. The soul who passionately loves anyone or anything else has committed adultery. Thus, to take pleasure in the world, to feel sensually involved, or to enjoy the life of the body is to have "loved another." Those who break out of the power structure of patriarchal marriage and its binary construction of gender have committed the worst form of sin: love of one's own kind instead of submission to one's superior.

If desiring intimacy with one's own kind is sin, then love for the world, for the earth from which we are made, is a disordered love. Everyone who passionately loves this earth is "queer."

When this theology rules—even subconsciously—lesbian, gay, bisexual, and transgender people are at risk. They are judged and treated as sinners whose very existence is an offense. The Bible is read as condemning all things queer, and salvation is associated with the secure maintenance of patriarchal, binary power structures.

Unless we can formulate a different understanding of sin, and with it a different vision of salvation, the oppression of bisexual, gay, lesbian, and transgender people will continue. We must go back and start again. We might begin by viewing sin as springing from fear, rather than from an inherently rebellious human nature. Fear of death, fear of isolation, fear of powerlessness, fear of threat—these feelings are visceral, deep, and compelling. Elementally, such feelings are life-protecting responses to a world in which so much threatens our survival and denies our self-worth. But in the struggle to get free from fear we can make destructive choices. Fearing powerlessness, we exert rigid control. Fearing rejection, we instigate hate. Fearing death, we arm ourselves to create death at will. Fearing isolation, we uncritically comply with the crowd or passively submit to others' needs and expectations. But these behaviors do not free us from fear. Rather, they create cultures that are rooted in fear and that pass on the inheritance of fear from one generation to the next.

Tragic mishandling of fear, helped along by structures of domination and submission, breeds alienation from ourselves, from one another, and from the earth. The brokenness of our lives because of sin is experienced as loneliness, helplessness, and worthlessness. Our relationships with one another are character-ized by power struggles and violence. This condition does not result from our personal depravity and lust; it is transpersonal. Even before we are born, cultures and histories are in place that will shape us to be afraid and will teach us how to handle fear. If we learn to channel fear into destructive patterns, injury and tragedy will be amplified in the world.

"Perfect love casts out fear," the Bible says in the first letter of John. If we understand that sin springs from fear, we can recog-nize that salvation must cast out fear and heal the wounds caused by fear-centered cultures. On a personal level, salvation from fear would mean experiencing a restored communion with all of life, a sense of creative power, and a deeply felt, joyful knowledge of one's intrinsic worth. Collectively, salvation would be embodied in cultures rooted in trust, cooperation, and respect for the power inherent in every creature. With sin and salvation reimagined in these ways, sex would not be the ultimate expression of sinfulness but a primary means of grace.

Beyond the garden of innocence, in which sin is defined as disobedience to the commands of God, there is another way to understand Eden. It is the garden of wisdom, in which earthly life is understood to be permeated by God's life-giving presence and adventures in loving become pathways to wholeness and liberation from fear. In the garden of wisdom, sexuality is a good gift, a source of joy, renewal, resistance, and spiritual illumination.

Making love can be a means of grace. Sexual intimacy can be a resource for the healing and transformation of life, a means through which we can restore our joy in being and our knowledge of our elemental goodness. It can give us awareness of our personal power to affect and be affected, our intimate connection with all of life, and our creative potency. This is not to say that sexuality is the only means of grace or that it automatically solves life's problems. There are other important means of grace—the world itself, the arts, friendship, rituals, meaningful work. And the goodness of sexuality can be undermined by any number of means: the use of sex to overpower or coerce others, sexual abuse of children by adults, the use of sex as a tool of manipulation, addiction to sexual intimacy as the exclusive source of one's sense of worth, sexual intimacy as a ritual reinforcement of domination and submission (as in traditional "Christian" marriage).

And there are times when, due to choice, circumstances, or age, sexual activity is not part of our lives. Childhood and early youth have other joys. We may find we must limit our sexual activity to protect our health or someone else's. Our sexual experiences may have been so traumatic that we find abstinence to be the most healing choice, itself a means of grace.

Furthermore, even our best sexual encounters are subject to human foibles or failures. We are blocked by fears and past hurts, insecurities, embarrassment, lack of confidence in our ability to give or receive pleasure, physical limitations, or illness. Satisfying sex may happen only now and then for us, if at all. Other pressing issues—both sorrows and joys—sometimes rightly take precedence in our attention. But, in its proper place and when it is not being abused, sex can be a means of grace, not only within the bounds of marriage or even within the bounds of committed relationship but in many forms.

The self-described positive sexual experiences of women form a body of literature that shows exactly how lovemaking can be a means of grace. Much of the available material on human sexuality reflects views formed in the context of patriarchal, heterosexist, gender-binary culture. New revelations emerge when we turn to voices and visions from outside the dominant culture, especially those of women—lesbian, bisexual, and straight—who have written about their most positive sexual experiences. The voices of transgender people further illuminate the grace possible in sexual intimacy.

One characteristic of this literature is a reluctance to isolate erotic experiences solely to sexual activity. Rather, erotic joy, as known in the best experiences of sexual enjoyment, becomes the touchstone of life. It reveals the ultimate possibilities of life, and the rest of life is judged against it. In Audre Lorde's view, the heights of sexual happiness become the foundation for ethics. In *Sister Outsider*, she writes,

> When we begin to live from within outward, in touch with the power of the erotic within ourselves, and allow that power to inform and illuminate our actions upon the world around us, then we begin to be responsible to ourselves in the deepest sense. For as we begin to recognize our deepest feelings, we begin to give up, of necessity, being satisfied with suffering and self-negation, and with the numbness which so often seems like their only alternative in our society. Our acts against oppression become integral with self, motivated and empowered from within.

This view of the erotic as the inner source of knowledge about fullness of life contrasts dramatically with the traditional Christian view of eros as destructive desire that leads to disobedience to God. In this positive view, carnal knowledge is not the Fall but the wellspring of right living, a resource for sustaining the vision of what is just and good, and a constant source that refreshes the desire for abundant life.

How might sexuality function, in Lorde's words, as "nursemaid of all our deepest knowledge"? For one thing, sexual intimacy can give us a profound sense of our communion with all of life, our connectedness in contrast to our loneliness or alienation. In love-making, we can feel boundaries falling away between the self and the world. One may feel as if the whole of life were flowing through one's body, or as if one were smelling, touching, tasting, and breathing the universe, or as if the self and the world were indistinguishable. This boundless sense of communion is the very thing that Augustine and Bonhoeffer found so offensive about sexuality. For them, the breakdown of a sense of limit signals estrangement from God and destruction of life, but it may in fact be the restoration of a healed sense of intimate connection to life.

In Susan Griffin's description, for example, making love approaches mystical enlightenment. In *Pornography and Silence*, she writes,

> If I let myself love, let myself touch, enter my own pleasure and longing, enter the body of another, the darkness, let the dark parts of my body speak, tongue into mouth, in the body's language, as I enter, a part of me I believed was real begins to die. I descend into matter, I know I am at the heart of myself, I cry out in ecstasy. For in love, we surrender our uniqueness and become world.

Describing this experience of sexual happiness as a merging with all of life, women use language similar to the language of mystical ecstasy, with images of profound stillness, whirling-dervish ecstasy, and brilliant light. This altered consciousness carries with it not only unbounded joy—an expansion of the self into a field of light or a depth of mystical darkness—but also matchless peace and life-renewing power.

Women also describe positive sexual encounters as experiences that heighten a sense of personal presence and power. Starhawk emphasizes this aspect of sexual intimacy when she writes in *Dreaming the Dark,*

> In sex we merge, give away, become one with another, allow ourselves to be caressed, pleasured, enfolded, allow our sense of separation to dissolve. But in sex we also feel our impact on another, we see our own faces reflected in another's eyes, feel ourselves confirmed, and sense our power, as separate human beings, to make another feel.

We feel ourselves felt. We know we are here, not invisible. We feel our power to give joy to another. We know our presence is a blessing to the world. We feel the joy the presence of the lover gives to us. We know soul to be the power of presence.

And if sexual intimacy shows us ourselves as a powerful presence and love as enjoyment of the presence of power of another, making love is a means of moving beyond a sense of ourselves as passive. It saves us from the sin of feeling helpless and empty, which leads to the horrible despair of believing we have no being. Lorde writes,

> In touch with the erotic, I become less willing to accept powerlessness, or those other supplied states of being which are not native to me, such as resignation, despair, self-effacement, depression, self-denial.

At its best, sexual intimacy teaches us this truth about ourselves: that joy is grounded in relational power. Thus, it frees us from the sin of pride (wanting to be completely in control) and the terror of despair (feeling ourselves to be completely powerless). It gives us courage to address injustice and brokenness in ourselves and our world. Rita Nakashima Brock explains it this way in *Journeys by Heart: A Christology of Erotic Power*:

> Our heartfelt action, not alone, but in the fragile, resilient interconnections we share with others, generates the power

that makes and sustains life. There, in the erotic power of the heart, we find the sacred mystery that binds us in loving each other fiercely in the face of suffering and pain and that empowers our witness against all powers of oppression and destruction.

Through loving and being loved, we can learn to embrace the gift of our own lives. We can begin to deeply honor ourselves and others. To honor ourselves profoundly is to live with receptivity to the world, accepting what it has given us and creatively responding in order to make greater justice and beauty, as an artist shapes a jar or composes a song.

Women describe a strong connection between sexual pleasure and creativity. Some associate sexual joy and creativity with their power to give birth. A woman describes a sexual fantasy in which she simultaneously gives birth and is made love to by her partner. A pregnant woman exclaims, "I feel so sexy, so fertile, full of energy, alive." Another woman says that during her daughter's birth she felt an overwhelming mystical connection to all life, a whole-body feeling of insight and ecstasy.

But the deeply felt tie between sexuality and creativity is not confined to women's experience of pregnancy and childbirth. Other experiences in which personal power is harnessed to bring forth life are felt to have erotic overtones as well. Whenever passion, energy, joy, personal power, and creativity emerge and converge, the experience can be felt as erotic. Starhawk defines the erotic as, simply, power from within. This power is carried within the body of every human being.

Sexual energy is life-giving energy. We know that all forms of giving life to life—giving life to ourselves, to another, to a work of imagination or research or a political cause—are bonded to sexual energy. Our pleasure grows throughout life the more we choose to create out of the power within us. We discover ourselves redeemed, healed, and restored. Minnie Bruce Pratt, in her book *S/he*, evokes this sacred return to wholeness and holiness, describing the simple happiness of a lover's presence:

You say that every night you will roll over and hold me, whisper in my sleeping ear that you love me, while urban lights stream like a galaxy of stars seen from a dark backyard. Every morning I will turn to you in the grey firstlight and you will say, "Good morning, angel," while city skyscrapers loom like a distant mountain range in the smog. We will wake in the light of a new creation, as if we have walked back into the garden, to have a room shadowed with trees of hibiscus and palm, a bed where we can briefly lie, side by side, with only the sunlight to clothe us.

Making love is not the be-all and end-all of life. It rarely approaches perfection, and it isn't the most important thing we do. But it is far from the root of all sin. On the contrary, it can be life's most delightful means of grace, reminding us of our creative power, our connection to all life, and our sheer delight in being. As such, it should be held in honor among all people, and no church or state should legislate against its potential for supporting all that is right, good, and joyful in our lives.

The Bible promises, "You shall be like a watered garden whose springs never run dry." It teaches that we can be part of the cascading streams by which "justice will flow down like waters and righteousness like an everflowing stream."

Most often, life is full of mundane tasks. Fear grinds our days into dust and ashes. But there are moments—and love-making can be one of them—when we experience a thirst-quenching downpour of unexpected grace, showering us in unmistakable, surprising joy. In such moments, like Valentine's Day, 2004, in San Francisco, the gates of the garden open, and we stand again on Eden's soil. New life begins once more, in love.

RECONSTRUCTING OUR FAITH

∞

CORNERSTONES

IN THE SPRING OF 2001, my ministerial colleague Lindi Ramsden asked if I would preach for her congregation at a special service to be held that coming fall. Their church in San Jose, California, had burned to the ground a few years earlier. After years of hard work, they were ready to dedicate the rebuilt sanctuary. I knew how heartbreaking the fire had been for them and how many obstacles they had overcome to raise their church from the ashes. It was time to celebrate. I said yes, and we set a date for mid-September, oblivious—as we all were—to the events that would dramatically alter the context of that celebration.

Over the summer, I thought about what I might say to them and decided I would build the sermon around the story of Jacob's dream. This ancient Jewish tale, recorded in Genesis, tells how the first shrine came to be. Jacob was on the road and, weary from travel, lay down to sleep on a mountain with only the stars overhead and a stone for his pillow. He dreamed of a ladder stretching up to the heavens, with angelic beings ascending and descending in a continuous flow of movement connecting heaven and earth. In his dream, Jacob heard a voice whisper a promise to him: "You and your children and your children's children will survive and be blessed." He woke up in awe and said, "There is holiness here! Surely this place is none other than the house of God, and this is the threshold of heaven!" To mark this place of revelation and promise, Jacob set up a stone and poured oil on it. He dedicated himself to the mysterious presence he had encountered and sealed his devotion by pledging 10 percent of his resources to God.

Thus are houses of worship built. They begin with a dream that holds something profound. For Jacob, it was a mystical sense that life is blessed and protected. Heaven is here, interpenetrating earth in a dynamic dance of divine energies connecting the stars above and the stones beneath.

For our religious ancestors who built the sanctuaries in which we gather, the dream was not dissimilar. Though they rejected Biblical literalism, our Unitarian and Universalist ancestors possessed a deep sense of the sacredness of the earth. They believed heaven was open before us—not a realm beyond earth or death. They saw that heaven was in the wildflowers and the night stars, in the stony mountains and the rushing streams. They saw, even more importantly, that heaven was in the quality of community they created. They placed their faith in the presence of divinity within human beings. "Heaven is in our hands," they said. With that sense of responsibility, they dedicated themselves to making the dream of heaven on earth a reality by working for justice, dignity, equality, religious tolerance, and freedom. They named this dream with the words they carved into the cornerstones of their sanctuaries: "To the worship of God and the service of man." These were the words, for example, engraved in the cornerstone of the First Unitarian Church of San Jose, California, first laid in 1865.

Satisfied that I had discovered the organizing principle for my sermon, I e-mailed the church my title and a brief description of the sermon so they could include it in their newsletter. I called my sermon "Cornerstones." It would lift up the human power to create heaven on earth and celebrate the sanctuary as the sacred container for that faith.

When two planes struck the World Trade Center on September 11, it was the human capacity to create hell—not heaven—that was vividly before our eyes. For days, we watched the tape over and over: one hundred and ten stories of steel collapsing—not once, but twice—folding life into death with a great clap of horror. When I finally returned to the task of preparing my sermon for the San Jose church, I knew it would have to change. How could we celebrate in the midst of this devastating sorrow? What could I, what *should* I, say to the congregation?

An article by *Time* senior editor Nancy Gibb provided a clue. Gibb referred to the World Trade Center as "our cathedral"—the sanctuary for our dreams as a nation. She knew she was treading on difficult ground when she characterized the events of September 11 as the destruction of our society's holy place, and she tried to disavow the troubling implications of her statement by adding that the values of the marketplace are not our true God. I set aside for a moment the questions that calling the World Trade Center our cathedral stirred up and stayed with the image: the collapse of the sanctuary, the destruction of the shelter for a dream.

In the aftermath of the devastation in New York and Washington, the media presented images of human heroism and love, touching stories that recalled us to human goodness, fragments of heaven drifting through the ruins of hell. We were grateful for the reassurance these images provided, but signs of human goodness did not inform the course our nation took in responding to the terrorist attack, and the political rhetoric that followed invoked neither tenderness nor human solidarity. Instead, we heard the language of war, vengeance, and retaliation. Fire, it appeared, was to be fought with fire.

People said the world changed on September 11, 2001. They said that America lost its innocence: Our dream had been shattered, a bubble of security and confidence had burst, and life in the United States would never be the same. But not everyone saw it this way. Before September 11, we lived in a world in which the human capacity to create hell on earth had been more than adequately revealed: the Holocaust, Hiroshima, Cambodia, Bosnia, Rwanda. What more evidence did we need to realize that we can destroy one another? People said such violence had never been known on American soil, but such statements overlooked the magnitude of our violent history. The Trail of Tears is a trail across American soil, a trail watered by the anguish of human faithlessness and betrayal. During the Middle Passage, American slave traders crowded people into the hulls of ships, chained and brutalized them, gave them minimal food and water, and carried them against their will to be slave laborers on American soil.

The rich earth of the country we ask God to bless was soaked with the blood of neighbor killing neighbor during the Civil War. September 11 did not match the magnitude of slaughter that occurred during even one day of that conflict. In his second inaugural address, Abraham Lincoln said that although people on each side offered prayers, God could not answer them. He said that war came because we, as a nation, had failed to end the evil of slavery. Lincoln did not console the nation with its innocence. He said we were fools to expect that we could engage in grave injustice and escape the consequences.

In the years since September 11, Americans have had to face up to our own society's capacity for harm. The violence of the terrorists who flew planes into the Pentagon and the World Trade Center is contemptible. And so is the violence that our own nation has employed against civilians, against children, against our own people, against prisoners of war. We bulldozed living human beings under the sand during Operation Desert Storm. We lobbed uranium-tipped bombs into the deserts of the Middle East, spreading environmental poison. We abused prisoners at Abu Ghraib and Guantanamo Bay. Integrity requires us to face ourselves honestly.

The rhetoric that paints our nation as standing for all that is good and righteous and our enemies as evil and insane misses the mark. Such rhetoric prevents us from asking the deeper questions that might turn us in the direction of peacemaking. Our religious communities can help us ask these deeper questions. We don't need any new reminders of human evil, any fresh shattering of our false innocence. What we need is to soberly assess ourselves and to examine again what we know about the things that make for peace. We need to rededicate ourselves to the values and the ways of living that create genuine security for all of Earth's people. Yes, we can create hell. But if, as our ancestors believed, we can also create heaven, what is the path we must follow to get there?

I realized that the people of the San Jose congregation could draw on their own history to lead them out of this difficult time. I reworked my sermon to remind them that what they learned in the aftermath of their fire could provide clues to how they might recover from the events of September 11. When the 1995 fire burned their sanctuary to the ground, nothing was left but charred ruins. Mercifully, there was no loss of life, and the devastation was an accident. But the sanctuary and all that it meant as a shelter for the spirit was destroyed. The night of the fire, the congregants gathered in the street. Stunned, they stood in puddles of water around the smoldering beams and fallen remnants of their former church home. A voice began to sing, then another. Soon their voices rose together singing a favorite hymn full of promise, not unlike the promise Jacob heard in his dream:

> Peace shall walk softly through these rooms,
> touching our lips with holy wine,
> till every casual corner blooms into a shrine.

In the moment of devastation, they resolved to restore the shelter for human hope that their ancestors had built. They pledged their faith to those who had come before them and those who would come after them. They took hands across the generations, and they held on. They grieved the loss and then went to work. They rallied and rebuilt. They rolled up their sleeves and painted. They got out their pocketbooks and wrote a check—and then another. They stayed late through meetings to hash out the details and choose the right direction. They were in it for the long haul. And while they did all this, they didn't neglect the church ministry that goes beyond stone and wood: education, pastoral care, worship, social witness. They created beauty from the ashes.

Not just the beauty of a resurrected building, but the beauty of a communion of people bound together by devotion to something that seemed impossible.

The congregation didn't just make a replica of the past. They rebuilt what was lost, but they created something new as well. In the floor of the sanctuary they made a labyrinth. Some say the labyrinth is a symbol of the Mother Goddess, the womb of life's creation. With its mystifying twists and turns, the labyrinth carries those who enter it to its heart. No matter where you are in the journey—even if looking ahead you can only see confusion, even if your face is turned away from your destination—you are on the path to the center. The labyrinth is an image of promise, a promise that no one who enters the sacred path is ever lost. It says that though the sacredness of life can be obscured, burned, and damaged, it is never completely lost. The Unitarian Church of San Jose today stands as a living witness that human dreams can be accomplished, hope and faith can carry people forward from the ashes, devastation can be transformed, and restoration achieved.

What about the rest of us? What is the lesson for us? In *You Can't Go Home Again*, Thomas Wolfe writes,

> Pain and death will always be the same. But under the pavements trembling like a pulse, under the buildings trembling like a cry, under the waste of time, under the hoof of the beast above the broken bones of cities, there will be something growing like a flower something bursting from the earth again, forever deathless, faithful, coming into life like April.

Such an affirmation is never easy to come by. It mostly comes to those who have seen the worst and then have seen beyond. Without denying the horror, the anguish, the power of destruction, they see something more. The week after September 11, Anthony Lane, the movie critic for the *New Yorker*, wrote a piece entitled "This Is Not a Movie," which ended with this reflection:

> The most important, if distressing, of the images to emerge from those hours are not of the raging towers, or of the

vacuum where they once stood; it is of the shots of people falling from the ledges, and, in particular, of two people jumping in tandem. It is impossible to tell, from the blur, what age or sex these two are, nor does that matter. What matters is the one thing we can see for sure: they are falling hand in hand. Think of Philip Larkin's poem about the stone figures carved on an English tomb, and the sharp tender shock of noticing that they are holding hands. . . . "What will survive of us is love."

It seems almost too fragile, this affirmation. The joined hands of people jumping to their deaths because, as one survivor who barely made it out of the World Trade Center said, "better to choose your death than be buried in the rubble." Hands clasped in mutual support and never letting go, not even in the free fall to the end—this act signals that human love has the power to survive destruction. In the midst of Europe's devastation at mid-twentieth century, the poet Rainer Maria Rilke wrote, "In the night we are all falling, falling, as the stars are all falling, yet there is one who holds all this falling."

Is this enough to save the world? I believe that it is. If the world is to be saved at all, it will be saved this way: bit by bit, in pieces here and there as human beings place their hands together, holding on through the terror to the end, offering the touch of companionship that reaches beyond horror to the assurance of faithful presence, an unbreakable fidelity that counters the infidelity of violence.

We can create heaven on earth. And when the old sanctuaries fall—as the World Trade Center did in 2001—we need to rebuild with something new as the cornerstone, something new woven into the pattern on the floor. Something that marks the awareness that love for one another is our only security. Faithful solidarity with one another on this planet is the only power that is stronger than violence and terror. Joining hands, working together to create beauty, risking for the sake of a future we hope for but cannot see, but still moving in the direction of what we dream can be.

Like the San Jose congregation, we can discover within our own experience the resources that will lead us from devastation to life. These resources are revealed in the stories of our lives and preserved in the wisdom of our religious traditions. The San Jose church laid a cornerstone that says "service," and down the street the Muslim center laid a cornerstone that says "God is one," and across town the synagogue laid a cornerstone that says "Love your neighbor as yourself." Next door the Baptists have laid a cornerstone that says "religious freedom," and the Methodists one that says "Do all the good you can," and the Catholics one that says "If you want peace work for justice." The Buddhists have laid a cornerstone that says "Practice compassion," and farther out in the valley, the Native Americans have assembled stones on which it is written, "Everything begins in Beauty. We are all children of one life." These are the cornerstones of hope.

Our task is to raise these cornerstones from the rubble of our failures and, in partnership with people down the block and around the world, to build and rebuild the foundations that make the promise to Jacob become a promise to all people: You and your children and your children's children will survive and be blessed. Let us shelter our dream that life can survive in blessing, and to that hope let us rededicate our resources and our lives.

Holy War and
Nonviolent Resistance

In a *Time* magazine article from February, 2002, columnist Johanna McGreary refers to the architects of the Bush administration's war in Iraq as "theologians," suggesting that their foreign policy was based more on faith than a clear foreign policy strategy. I was surprised to see *Time* calling the White House political and military advisors theologians, but I don't disagree. Their theology is constructed around a claim that violence is an adequate path to redemption. What are the theological sources of such a claim and how can religion either contribute to or resist war?

War cannot be denied as a powerful force for meaning. It intensifies bonds of love; witness the touching scenes of military families saying goodbye to loved ones boarding planes to be deployed to the Middle East. It generates a strong sense of community that makes differences petty or unimportant; witness how Congress set aside differences to unite behind the president in the days following September 11. It moderates the sting of lives lost with the satisfaction of knowing death came as a result of courage and generosity; notice how often we have heard the emotional intensity of the words, "He died in the line of duty, seeking to protect others." It creates a sense of pride and accomplishment for individuals and nations; we stopped Hitler; we liberated the people of Afghanistan; we stood up to the bullies. It sanctifies submission to a higher authority, relieving the anxiety and boredom created by liberal ideologies of autonomy and the pursuit of happiness. In short, war assures us that we do not live—or die—in vain.

Chris Hedges, a war correspondent for fifteen years, gives personal witness to war's appeal. In his recent book, *War Is a Force That Gives Us Meaning*, he tells of his own seduction by the intensity and supreme sense of purpose found on the battlefield. He admits that violence has an addictive power. Violence produces an adrenaline rush that overwhelms ordinary consciousness and sense experience, creating a high that has qualities of ecstasy. But, like other addictions, the joy of battle splits ecstasy off from the realities of what actually happens to bodies, communities, land, and culture when war takes place. Underneath the valor, those who see war up close encounter a vast emptiness. The force of war's meaning crumbles in its real presence.

War extracts a very high price for the sense of significance it can offer. It depends on the sacrifice of life, both during war and after. After the Vietnam War, for example, suicide among veterans claimed more U. S. lives than the war itself. Those who serve in active combat often experience long-term psychological and physical suffering. This suffering extends into family systems and communities, where homelessness and poverty among veterans run high. War also sacrifices the environment by poisoning soil and water, burning forests, destroying habitats, and disrupting agriculture. Since the first Gulf War, there has been a sharp rise in birth defects and cancer rates in southern Iraq. The lack of clean water caused by the targeted destruction of water systems, the embargo on chlorine, and the use of depleted uranium weaponry has led to widespread disease. The United Nations estimates that, as a result, 500,000 Iraqi children died between 1991 and 2003.

In the end, war takes away the gift it gives. Its meaning can only be sustained if we deny, ignore, or forget suffering children, devastated veterans and their families, decimated cultures, and damaged ecosystems. Hedges quotes J. Glenn Gray, a veteran of World War II: "The great god Mars tries to blind us when we enter his realm, and when we leave he gives us a generous cup of the waters of Lethe to drink." A society can forget or hide what it knows.

As a parish minister, I learned that accurate and integrated memory can be an important mode of resistance to war. The Social Concerns Committee wanted the church to raise public awareness of the growing stockpile of nuclear weapons in the world. One member of the Committee, Mary Brown, suggested that we place posters on the city's fleet of buses. The posters would depict the increase in stockpiles of nuclear weapons since the end of World War II. Not everyone thought this was a good idea, especially the older members of the church.

The topic came up again at the women's Bible class that week. The women grumbled about how the church was spending too much of its energy working on political issues. Why should we be raising questions about military strategy? It wasn't our place. One woman called a halt to the debate. "Just a minute," she said. "How can you say we have no place having an opinion about this?" She looked around at the women in the group. "Every one of us here knows that our men came home from World War II broken," she said quietly. "We've spent our lives holding together the pieces that war broke. We did our best to take care of them as well as our children. And never speaking of it, always saying it was a good war. We know there is no such thing as a good war." There was quiet in the room as one by one the women silently nodded, remembering. After that, the women in the class supported Mary Brown's project. The church printed the posters and filled the city's buses with them.

Without memory, society can succumb to war's false promise; the drama and seduction of war can return. Today in the U. S. we are seeing a renaissance of desire for war. This is happening, in part, because we have allowed ourselves to forget what we know, what we have seen, what we have experienced of war and its aftermath.

To recognize that war is a force that gives life meaning is to reveal its relationship to another force that gives life meaning, religion. Every major religion on the planet has, at one time or another, provided religious justification for war. As Mark Juergensmeyer ably demonstrates in his important book, *Terror in the Mind of God*, it is neither fair nor historically accurate to identify religiously sanctioned violence with only one or two of the world's religious systems while regarding others as peaceable.

Juergensmeyer studies religious terrorists around the world, from white supremacist Christians in the U. S. who carried out the Oklahoma City bombing, to Buddhists in Japan who released poisonous gas in a Tokyo subway station, to Jewish and Palestinian terrorists, to Hindu and Islamic terrorists. Juergensmeyer interviews religious terrorists and concludes that religious ideas create systems of meaning within which the action of terrorists is rational and virtuous. He notes surprisingly similar themes across the boundaries of diverse religious faiths. The holy warrior sees the world in black-and-white, with good and evil arrayed in stark opposition. The warrior's people have been attacked, injured, or humiliated in some way, and payback is in order. Salvation, peace, and blessing will be established by those who—in faithfulness to a higher calling, an illuminated mind, or the power of God working through them—are willing to risk everything in order to avenge wrongs or destroy evil.

Juergensmeyer comments that there is little that can match the power of holy war as a system of meaning. Holy war provides a complete and comprehensive picture of the world; it explains the meaning of history and projects an ultimate triumph of goodness. It gives the holy warrior a transcendent purpose, to which even the loss of one's life pales in comparison. This transcendent purpose requires using violence to destroy or debilitate evil, but such destruction is performed in service to or in intimate relationship with a transcendent source of power. The violent actor is united with divinity. A more intense system of meaning can hardly be found.

My own work as a theologian has focused on analyzing the dominant religious tradition in the United States, Christianity. I study Christianity as a Christian; it is my heritage. I have chosen to wrestle with its blessings and its curses, and I seek to be guided by its best wisdom while contributing to its repentance and ongoing reformation. I also approach my religious commitment as a humanist, placing higher value on reasoned observation of the world and critical reflection on experience than on received tradition, creed, or sacred scriptures.

I believe that for our society to embrace peacemaking more fully we—even those who do not identify as Christians—need to understand more deeply the religious heritage that a majority of Americans align themselves with. We need a keen awareness of how Christian theologies have promoted holy war and sanctioned violence, especially through theologies of the cross.

During its first millennium, Christianity focused its sights on paradise, resurrection, and the living presence of Christ. The cross was a ubiquitous image in Christian art during those years, but it was always depicted as a resurrection cross—a sign of the promise of life. The cross appears blossoming into a spiraling green tree, issuing forth cascades of water flowing from the Garden of Eden, bursting into a sun at dawn, or glittering in a midnight blue sky filled with gold and silver stars. But virtually nowhere during the first thousand years of Christian art do we find the cross depicted with a man nailed to it, dying an anguished death. The first appearance of a monumental image of Jesus dying on the cross can be dated to the end of the tenth century, in Northern Europe.

After nearly a millennium of absence, the emergence of the dead Christ as an icon for Christian meditation marked a major shift in Christianity—a shift toward violence. Earliest Christian practice forbade Christians from taking up arms of any kind or serving in the military. In the second century, Justin Martyr writes in *Dialogue with Trypho*, "We ourselves are well conversant with war, murder, and everything evil, but all of us throughout the whole wide earth have traded in our weapons of war."

Of course, this did not last. Early Christianity's disavowal of the use of violence was gradually eroded, especially by the changes that began when Constantine professed that a dream of the cross gave him the power to defeat Maxentius at the Milvian Bridge in 311, giving him control of the Roman West. Bishop Ambrose of Milan and Augustine of Hippo provided theological justification for the use of violence by Christians. By 438, the Theodosian Code reversed the church's early practice and mandated that none could serve in the Roman army—but Christians. Despite this change in attitude toward the military, violence was still regarded as a necessary evil, not a good. Soldiers who killed were required to do penance.

But in the tenth century, Europe was experiencing a breakdown in the power of kings to enforce law and maintain peace. The Carolingian Empire was in decline, and local castellans used violence to plunder the countryside, robbing monasteries and attacking travelers. In the absence of secular powers that kept the peace, bishops began to call peace councils, demanding that the castellans take vows not to destroy church property. When these vows proved inadequate, church officials found it necessary to recruit armed soldiers into the service of the church. In *Crusading Peace*, Tomaz Mastnak explains,

> By setting rules specifying whom arms-bearers were not allowed to attack, the kinds of property they were not allowed to touch, and days of the week and seasons of the year when they were not allowed to use arms, the peace council regulations also gave the church the authority to determine who could employ arms, for what purpose, on whose command, against whom, and when. The circumscription of violence opened the way for the Church not only to assert its control over the use of arms but also to direct violent action.

In November 1095, Pope Urban II called a peace council in Clermont, France. Preaching to the massed gathering of armed nobles, bishops, monks, and laity, he called them to turn aside from fighting one another and turn instead to fighting against the enemies of Christ in the East. In *The Preaching of the Crusades*, Penny J. Cole comments that Pope Urban argued strongly for the unprecedented and extraordinary character of the war which he was proposing: one instigated by God, in which the combatants were not plunderers but soldiers of Christ fighting not improperly but rightly, and whose reward was not to be a few coins but eternal glory and friendship with God. As preparation, they were to receive, by Christ's command, the remission of their sins.

Scholars of the Crusades point out that the instigating factors of this first crusade were not to be found at Europe's borders; Muslims were a minimal threat. The issues were within the sphere of Europe's social, political, and religious concerns. In service to those concerns, Pope Urban characterized Muslims in the east as godless, violent filth, as enemies of God.

Thousands responded to Urban's sermon by "taking up the cross." In public rallies, they vowed to give their lives in the service of God's honor. At first, however, they did not travel east. They traveled north to the Rhineland and began to hunt and kill Jews. In *Constantine's Sword*, James Carroll quotes a medieval Hebrew chronicler explaining what it meant when a preacher of the Crusades arrived in Trier during Passover in the spring of 1096: "When he came here, our spirit departed and our hearts were broken and trembling seized us and our holiday was transformed into mourning."

The crusaders pursued, tormented, and killed approximately ten thousand Jews in the Rhineland in the spring of 1096—nearly a third of the Jewish population in Europe. This was the first large-scale massacre of Jews by Christians. By 1099, the crusading Christian armies had reached Jerusalem. The account of their conquest of the city by eyewitness Raymond of Aguilers, quoted in Tomaz Mastnak's *Crusading Peace*, bears witness to the extent to which violence in the name of God led to atrocities:

> Piles of heads, hands, and feet were to be seen in the streets of the city. . . . Indeed, it was a just and splendid judgment of God, that this place should be filled with the blood of unbelievers, since it had suffered so long from their blasphemies.

A Muslim chronicle from this period tells of refugees from the atrocities in Jerusalem arriving in Baghdad during Ramadan. It describes the weeping in the mosques as the refugees' stories were told. The chronicle reports that the distress of the refugees was so great that they were relieved from observing the fast. War became a force that gave life meaning and strengthened the "peace" among Christians at the expense of those who would be required to fulfill the role of enemy: Jews, Muslims, and heretics. Interpretations of the meaning of Christ's death were central to the preaching of the crusades. Crusaders vowed to avenge the death of Christ, to defend Christ's kin in his name, to offer themselves as he did in obedience and faith to God, as a sacrificial offer that merited a reward.

Anselm of Canterbury, Pope Urban's friend, provided the formal theology that captured the spirit of the age. Writing in 1096, in the midst of the first crusade, he produced *Cur Deus Homo*, "Why God Became Human"—the first full-blown explication of the doctrine that Jesus' death on the cross saved humanity. Anselm's substitutionary theory of the atonement interprets Christ's death on the cross as payback to God for humanity's debt of sin. Anselm writes, "Man absolutely cannot give himself more fully to God than when he commits himself to death for God's honor." He exhorts Christians to imitate Christ's self-offering when the cause of God's justice demands it.

In Anselm's theology, God was honored by Jesus' execution, and the boundless merit of Jesus' suffering blesses all Christians. With this theology, Western Christianity embraced violence as pleasing to God. Violence was no longer a sin that required penance; it was holy. Christian holy war became a penitential act. The fastest route to paradise was to kill or be killed. Self-sacrifice became the highest love, and death by torture became salvation. God was imagined to take pleasure in the murder of human beings.

Mastnak sees in this first crusade a blurring of boundaries, a failure to distinguish realities. The *pax Dei* movement had confused temporal and eternal peace. In calling for the Crusade, Urban confused heavenly and earthly Jerusalem. Likewise, the acts of violence committed by the crusaders confused the historical actors who killed Jesus with present Jews and Muslims who had lived peacefully with Christians and confused the mystical body of Christ with the literal body of the dead Jesus. The iconography of the crucified Christ provided a visual point of reference in which these confusions merged into one multivalent image.

Psychological studies of violence point to the ways in which a blurring of boundaries comes into play in acts of extreme violence. Present realities become substitutes for other realities; the target of violence becomes a stand-in for someone or something else. Times, places, and people merge. Mass violence, in particular, fails to distinguish realities and excels at false identifications. It creates meaning by force of false associations that have come to seem completely rational.

The substitutionary theory of the atonement generates a series of substitutions. Crusaders slaughtered Jews, who substituted for Muslims, who substituted for earlier "Jews" accused of killing Christ, who substituted for the Romans, who actually killed Christ. Jesus substitutes for sinful humanity to pay the debt owed God. God substitutes for Satan as the cause of Jesus' death. Personal suffering and self-sacrifice substitute for the moral virtues of self-restraint and serenity. And committing violence substitutes for spiritual rebirth as the route to paradise.

This theology, like violence, obliterates distinctions and replicates itself indiscriminately. Now, Afghanistan can substitute for al Qaeda. Saddam Hussein can substitute for Osama Bin Laden, or Saddam Hussein can substitute for Hitler. Iraq can substitute for Afghanistan. Palestinians can substitute for Nazis. Any Muslim can substitute for any terrorist.

The publication of *Cur Deus Homo* and the emergence of the crucifix as an image for devotion mark the beginning of a thousand-year period in Western history dominated by the confusion of violence, self-sacrifice, and love. The inability to distinguish among them becomes explicit in the piety of crusading. To engage in a military campaign in defense of Christ's people against the unbelievers came to be regarded as an act of great love. In *The Crusades: A History*, Jonathan Riley-Smith writes that Cardinal Odo of Chateauroux preached a crusade organized in 1245 with these words:

> It is a clear sign that a man burns with love of God and zeal for God when he leaves country, possessions, house, children and wife, going overseas in the service of Jesus Christ. . . . Whoever wishes to take and have Christ ought to follow him: to follow him to death.

This is the theology that haunts us still in legacies of war as a force that gives life meaning. In the U. S. today, forms of Christian piety abound in which faithfulness to Jesus is equated with willingness to die defending one's country or willingness to sacrifice our young people in order to liberate others from evil. When Osama Bin Laden speaks of the U. S. war agenda as a crusade, he is tragically accurate. The impulse to destroy the infidels and to regard doing so as an act of love for God is a present reality in U. S. culture. It may not be the motivating factor for Bush and his advisors. Additional pernicious agendas, such as gaining greater control of the world's oil fields, must be taken into account. And it doesn't mean the problems of terrorism and global security aren't real. They are. But the Bush administration sounds the notes of holy war in subtle and pervasive ways. It relies on the presence in U. S. society of a large number of people for whom war is a religious act, an act of faith, hope, courage, and love.

When, as a parish minister, I began to preach about the link between theologies of atonement and violence, many illustrative stories surfaced in my Seattle congregation. Some of the most powerful were the stories of men's experience of war. The devastating consequences of war for those who serve in active combat were made clear to me by parishioners breaking their long silences about the realities of combat. So too were the resources that people found to put life back together in the aftermath of violence, even when it took a long time.

Bill and Marge were long-time members of the congregation I served in Seattle. One day, Bill asked me to come see him. He'd been diagnosed with an inoperable brain tumor. "I want you to hear my testimony before I die," he'd said on the phone. Bill and Marge lived out of town in a small house shaded by trees, close to the edge of the lake. There was a quietness there, and I felt the warmth of their home when I settled in by the fire. Marge disappeared into some other part of the house. We all knew that the brain tumor was far advanced, but Bill could still talk cogently.

"I'm not afraid to die," Bill began. "I want you to know that. And I want you to hear why. I was in the Korean War. They made me a sergeant and gave me a group of men to command. They were good guys. I loved them. Every one of them. Especially Sam, my best buddy. He was sweet and honest. He never said a hurtful word. He was always there when you needed him. We made it through some tough spots in that jungle. But the men were getting tired. Run down with sickness, the heat.

"One day, a message came through from my commanding officer, ordering us to make an ambush the next day. I knew where we were in the jungle. I knew where the enemy was. I knew if we made the ambush, there was no chance that we could succeed at the objective or get out alive. It was a suicide mission.

"I argued with the commanding officer. I told him the mission would fail, and that it was a stupid idea to send us in there. I went so far as to tell him that even if he gave the order, I would refuse to lead my men into there. He told me I was betraying my duty as a soldier, that I was letting personal feelings get in the way of my responsibility, that if I wasn't going to carry out the command I wasn't an American, I wasn't a soldier, I wasn't a man. I felt ashamed of myself for questioning. The next day, I gave the order. We went at it. It was bad." Bill stopped speaking for a moment, composing himself. "Most of my men were killed."

Bill hunched over and wrapped his arms around himself. "I was holding Sam in my arms when he died." It was quiet for a moment. "I broke down then." I wasn't good for anything anymore. They sent me home. In my eyes, I had failed in every way. I had questioned my superior officer. I had faltered in doing my duty. And when my men were killed, I couldn't take the pain. I began to drink. I wanted the pain to go away. I drank for the next twenty years. My family fell apart. My wife and children were disappointed in me. Angry. Hurt. She took them and left. I drank more. Slowly but surely I was killing myself.

"Then I met Marge." Bill sat up, caught my eye, and smiled. "Marge was tough. She told me I was worth something but I was treating myself like shit. She knew; she'd been there. Thanks to Marge's love I got into AA. I stopped drinking. I began to feel all the things I'd buried and think all the things I couldn't bear to think. It was rough, but the other guys in AA listened to all the crap I had to say about myself, about the world. They just listened. Didn't tell me I was right. Didn't tell me I was wrong. Didn't blink. Then I really began to come to my senses, like the Bible says.

"I saw the truth. Back there in Korea, I was right to have questioned my commanding officer. I was right to feel the order should be disobeyed. And when I broke down because my buddies died, I was right to cry."

As Bill spoke, he placed both his hands on his own chest. "This is my manhood," he said, tapping a rhythm with his hands upon his body. "That I can feel. That I can care. That I can grieve. That I can love. That I hate war. That I had the courage to question. That I was willing not to obey. I'm not afraid to die now, because I know what love is. I know where God is." His hand again, pressing against his flesh. "This is what I wanted you to hear from me before I die." He took my young hands in his old ones and looked at me. "It is important for you to know this. You are a preacher. Tell my story. People need to know what I'm telling you. You need to know what I'm telling you."

Bill had hated himself. But his life had been saved by a listening community, the tough encouragement of his wife, and by something in himself that rebelled against the suppression of his capacity to think, feel, and act.

Effective resistance to violence begins with our personal efforts to integrate our experiences and knowledge of violence and its effects on our lives. Like Bill, we may need to find a new path or a new heart or discover a new identity. Effective resistance to violence expands through the work of communities and their capacities to enable recovery, to find some means of restitution, to negotiate responses to violence within a vision of restorative justice, and to bear witness to the sustaining power of love. Such communities of remembrance, resistance, and hope enable human thriving amidst all the powers arrayed against them in their own times and places.

A few weeks before the U. S. invasion of Iraq, millions of people from every age, race, religion, occupation, and social background demonstrated—in four hundred cities around the world, under conditions of icy winds, balmy skies, pouring rains, and scorching heat—to prevent a preemptive U. S. strike. The isolation of the U. S. among the people of the world in that winter of discontent was, perhaps, a small glimmer of hope that the last nuclear century helped us see that we must pull back from the abyss, that violence is never a solution, and that we are all in this together. None of us can save the world alone. But together—face-to-face, present to life's beauty and terror, to our power to harm as well as heal, and in reverence to that power within us that rebels against the suppression of our capacity to think, feel, and act—together, we can create peace.

What They Dreamed
Is Ours to Do

At its simplest, *covenant* means to come together. More precisely, it means to come together by making a promise, as when two people promise to love and care for one another. Unitarian Universalists often speak of covenant as a verbal statement of promise between individuals who, exercising their freedom of choice, bring community into being. There are historical reasons why we think this way. It is an expression of the dominance of an individualistic understanding of human existence. First comes the individual, then the community.

But our times demand that we think in other ways about the relationship between the individual and the community. The limits of a merely individualistic understanding of human existence are pressing upon us. Our attachment to an economic system that maximizes self-interest has broken our covenant with the earth and with one another. As a religious movement, we must grapple with what this means, including taking a hard look at the complicity of our religious tradition in this broken covenant. It is important that we do this. Multiple oppressions that our hearts cry out against—racism, sexism, the neglect of children, the abuse of the environment—intersect in an economic system in which the bottom line is individual self-interest.

The theological history of covenant can help us see another way, offering clues to how we might repair the promises we have broken.

In 1990, I moved to California to become president of the Starr King School for the Ministry. Truth be told, I was feeling proud of myself. Captain of my ship and master of my soul, I had valiantly charted my course to become first a cellist, then a minister, and now an educator.

When I got to California, I discovered I had a passel of distant cousins I had never met. One of them, my cousin Eldon Ernst, was dean of the American Baptist Seminary at the Graduate Theological Union in Berkeley. He proposed an Ernst family reunion, and so we got together. When we arrived in the driveway of cousin Jane Ernst's home, my first impression of my distant cousins came from reading the bumper stickers on their cars. One said, "If you want peace, work for justice." Another, "Teachers do it with class." Another, "Live music is best." And then there was one that said, "If you love Jesus, tithe."

Inside, over Jell-O salad, homemade rolls, and tuna casserole reminiscent of every church potluck I had ever attended, we said hello to one another. Here was Jane, a minister of religious education and graduate of the Pacific School of Religion. Here was Mike, a professional French horn player and high school music teacher, and Eldon, a seminary dean, and David, a United Methodist parish minister. Every single one of my distant cousins was a musician, minister, or teacher—and several were all three. Not only that, the ministers were all liberal social activists with an intellectual bent, and all the musicians were classical.

Apparently, I had never made any choices at all! I did not make myself; my life was given to me. And this is how it is: We receive who we are before we choose who we will become. As human beings, our lives begin and never leave the soil of this earth that shapes us through blood, kinship, genes, culture, associations, social systems, networks of relationships, and extended communities. Even when we do not directly know the people whose lives are linked with ours, our lives unfold in relationship to theirs.

This is how it is with covenant as well. We are born into relationships before we shape them by our conscious intention. We inherit covenant before we create covenant. We are given the gift of life, the gift of the earth that sustains life, the gift of one another and of all the generations leading up to now. As the hymn by Brian Wren says,

> We are not our own,
> Earth forms us,
> Human leaves on nature's growing vine,
> Fruit of many generations,
> Seeds of life divine.

Covenant making must begin with these questions: What have we been given? What is the covenant we are already in?

In his book *Puritanism and Liberty*, A. S. P. Woodhouse describes the vision of English clergyman Robert Browne. In the sixteenth century, Browne, inspired by the Reformation, drew on the Biblical image of promise making between God and his people to propose a revolution in church life. Churches should come into being, he said, as a covenant among persons, but not through common assent to a doctrine or through sacraments administered by priests hierarchically arrayed and apostolically descended. Instead, people should join themselves by a mutual agreement to walk together, to keep Christ's commandments, to choose their ministers and teachers, to put forth and debate questions, to learn the truth, and to welcome the voices of protest, complaint, and dissent. Browne hoped for a church in which people would mutually agree "that any might protest, appeal, complain, exhort, dispute, reprove . . . watch for disorders, reform abuses, and debate matters." Four hundred and fifty years later, we are the fulfillment of Browne's dream. Our present-day character was shaped by a vision long ago. It is important for us to remember that we are, first of all, relational beings shaped by history and by a community of faith. Our exercise of free choice takes place in the context of relational existence.

The early theologians of covenantal church life knew this. They spoke of the Covenant of Grace. They said that God, by the workings of grace, created the community of regenerated souls. Human action in making a church covenant merely makes visible what the Creator of Life has already done by giving human beings the gift of life and empowering us to be together in freedom and peace. Explicit covenant making is a human response to a gift from a source larger than ourselves. James Luther Adams emphasizes this in his book, *The Prophethood of All Believers.*

> Traditionally our churches have been grounded in a covenant binding us together . . . but this enterprise of maintaining the network is itself not to be understood as simply a human enterprise. It is a response to a divinely given creative power, a sustaining power, a community-transforming power. This power is ultimately not of our own making.

There is room to imagine this source larger than ourselves in multiple ways: Earth itself, the Spirit of Life, God, the Buddha nature, the communion of all souls, universal love. The point is that there is a power that supports our covenant making that is more than the power of our will and decision making. In fact, our covenant making is a response to this power, a collaboration with it.

The poet Rumi says, "If they say there is no communion without words, tell them, 'I have heard that lie before.'" Fundamentally, covenant is not a verbal agreement but a practice. It is formed by coming together in peace and committing ourselves as coworkers with the source of life. The Cambridge Platform of 1648 defined the principles of covenantal church life in New England. The Platform says,

> Real agreement and consent they do express by their constant *practice* in coming together for the public worship of God, and by their religious subjection unto the ordinances of God . . . not only by word of mouth, but by sacrifice . . . and also, sometimes, by silent consent, without any writing, or expression of words at all.

Woodhouse quotes the Puritan Richard Mather echoing these

sentiments in 1644. Mather wrote that covenant may be implied by "constant and frequent acts of communion performed by a company of Saints joined together by cohabitation in towns and villages . . . the falling in of their spirits into communion in things spiritual." What a lovely phrase: *the falling in of their spirits into communion.* This dimension of covenant is important for us to recover. It is an antidote to our radical individualism. We need this older sense of covenant as created by grace and sustained by practice. Our verbal promises are the frosting on the cake, not the cake itself. They may help us keep the covenant we are in, but they are not the covenant itself. By our acts of worshipping in a Unitarian Universalist congregation; structuring our life together to give room for the experience, voice, and vote of each person; and joining together to resist injustice, our spirits have fallen into communion.

We've fallen into communion with the feisty, free-spirited Puritans of 450 years ago, who advocated freedom of religious conscience and resisted the oppressive powers of church and state. We've fallen into communion with the people who believe revelation is not sealed. John Robinson's words to the departing Pilgrims echo in us still: "The Lord hath more truth yet to break forth. . . . I beseech you remember it as an article of your church covenant that you be ready to receive whatever truth shall be made known to you." We've fallen into communion with the sweet-spirited Universalists of old, who rejected a notion of God as a tyrant ruling by the threat of hell and named God as a gracious, creative presence who saves all through the power of love. We've fallen into communion with the deep-feeling Transcendentalists, who insisted that religion cannot be found in the dry bones of the past but must be discovered firsthand.

We've fallen into communion with the Iowa Sisterhood and all those who have advocated for the rights and full humanity of women. We've fallen into communion with the all-embracing mystics who see truth manifest in the diverse religious traditions of earth's people and mystery revealed in the trees and the stars. And we've fallen into communion with courageous Humanists who dare to lift up the dignity and strength of human beings, the power and importance of critical reason, in a world that prefers the abrogation of human agency and uncritical obedience to false gods. We live within this communion of souls and receive the beauty given to us by their lives, so closely linked with ours. This is the covenant we are already in.

I suggest that what we have received from this covenant is, most of all, membership in a community of resistance to oppression. Let us wake up into the dream they dreamed, of abundant life for all, and in our time put into practice the way of life that will embody the realization of that dream.

Consider the words of English Puritan Richard Overton in 1647, quoted in *Puritanism and Liberty*:

> It is a firm law and radical principle in nature, engraved in the tables of the heart by the finger of God in creation, for every living, moving thing, wherein there is the breath of life, to defend, preserve, guard, and deliver itself from all things hurtful, destructive and obnoxious thereto, to the utmost of its power. Therefore from hence is conveyed to all men in general, and to every man in particular, an undoubted principle of reason, by all rational and just ways and means possible he may save, defend, and deliver himself from all oppression, violence and cruelty.

The Free Church tradition emerged in the sixteenth century as part of a reforming movement that resisted the corrupt hierarchical power of the church and the economic alliance between the feudal aristocracy and the church. The making of church covenants asserted the power of people to determine their own lives and to choose who would govern them. It was a grassroots empowerment movement that became a decisive factor in the rise of modern democracy and the emergence of a postfeudal economic system.

In the presence of injustice and oppression, our forebears embraced freedom. They advocated for free speech, dissent, open debate, and tolerance of different opinions in a disciplined search for truth. Freedom of speech was important, not only as an end in itself but as a means to social change. They challenged economic systems that neglected the poor, justice systems that were unfair, prison systems that were cruel, and economic practices that concentrated wealth in the hands of a few.

The covenant of which we are part is a tradition that resists oppression by directly challenging the authority of oppressors, acting to remove them from power, and establishing new structures or alternative communities that put what is hoped for into practice. Most importantly, in this covenant, oppression is resisted finally not by argument, not by protest marches, not by passing resolutions, but by the practices of covenanted church life.

Betty Reid Soskin, a contemporary Unitarian Universalist community activist, articulates this radical principle this way, paraphrasing Gandhi: "The way to change the world is to be what we want to see." Quaker Jim Corbett, leader of the Sanctuary movement, speaks of this as civil initiative. In contrast to civil disobedience, civil initiative brings about change by proposing and manifesting, more than by dismantling and opposing.

Our Puritan forebears resisted oppression by putting into practice a way of life that demonstrated an alternative to structures of oppression. This was the heart of their covenant: to be what they wanted to see, to live as if the day of justice had arrived. They organized their church life to include the free conscience of each individual in a mutual commitment to the common good. They manifested an alternative to the oppressive use of power by a small elite that was uninterested in the welfare of all and that exercised economic and religious power without consent or accountability.

As matters evolved, what the Puritans first practiced in their congregations transformed nations. Woodhouse remarks,

> The congregation was the school of democracy. There the humblest member might hear, and join in the debate, might witness the discovery of the natural leader, and participate in that curious process by which there emerges from the clash of many minds a vision clearer and a determination wiser than any single mind could achieve.

A survey of Unitarian Universalists undertaken in 1998 by the Fulfilling the Promise Task Force asked, "What are your dreams for the UU movement?" A strong majority said our highest hope is to "become a visible and influential force for good in the world." The history of covenant making shows that the means for tremendous influence for the common good are in our hands. We do not need more money, though it always helps when we are as liberal regarding money as we are in other matters. We do not need more people, though it would be good to have them, and many in our society need what congregational life can give. To be an influential force for good, what we need to do is establish more strongly in our congregational life the practices that embody loving, just, and sustainable community. We need to be what we want to see and make visible an alternative to the forms of oppression, alienation, and injustice that characterize our time.

Doing so will be a form of keeping faith with the covenant we are already in—the covenant of resistance to oppression. Not doing so will be to break covenant with those who came before us, who built the house we gratefully inhabit. I am reminded of the great Unitarian Universalist hymn, "Rank by Rank Again We Stand."

> Though the path be hard and long,
> Still we strive in expectation;
> Join we now their ageless song
> One with them in aspiration.
> One in name, in honor one,
> Guard we well the crown they won:
> What they dreamed be ours to do,
> Hope their hopes and seal them true.

It is exciting to contemplate what might be asked of us and what promise we might fulfill, if we take this task seriously and give our lives to it. But it will take courage, spiritual stamina, and strength. To find it, we will have to take a path that we may not want to follow. We will have to look at the complicity of our religious tradition in the failure of our society to be just and sustainable.

The history of covenant making shows us that covenants can fail, break, or be severely compromised. In our time, the broken covenant we live with is loss of love for our neighbors and care for the earth. The dismantling of welfare, the increasing gap between rich and poor, the marginalization of the most disadvantaged, and the abuse of the environment are profound social failures. This broken covenant has come about through economic practices unsuccessfully checked by values beyond individual gain. The covenantal tradition that we claim as our own has tragically helped to bring this about. We are implicated in the deep intertwining of radical individualism and economic self-interest. Robert Bellah named this for us in an address he gave at the 1998 General Assembly of the Unitarian Universalist Association of Congregations:

> Almost from the beginning the sacredness of the conscience of the individual person was linked to the right to pursue one's own economic interests. . . . It is no accident, as they say, that the United States, with its high evaluation of the individual person, is nonetheless alone among North Atlantic societies in the percentage of our population who live in poverty, and that we are dismantling what was already the weakest welfare state of any North Atlantic nation. . . . And this is in no small part due to the fact that our religious individualism is linked to an economic individualism which, ultimately, knows nothing of the sacredness of the individual.

Naming our dilemma is a start. But how will we find the spiritual resources to purify our souls? What will it take for us to untangle our deepest religious values—the sacredness of the individual and the importance of freedom—from their alliance with an economic system that is failing the poor and threatening the earth? What must we do to find a new heart, unfettered by the false alliance of freedom with greed?

A final story from the history of covenantal theology provides some clues to a way ahead. The first great failure of Puritan covenantal life happened in 1649 in England. The Puritans had led a movement to reform English society on a number of fronts: to end abuses of power by the monarch and to advocate for land reform, prison reform, alleviation of poverty, unjust laws, burdensome taxes, debtors' prisons, and others. Fueled by the power of covenant making and the principles of freedom of conscience, free speech, and open debate and dissent, they rode a tide of hope and put their love of freedom and their opposition to oppression into dramatic action.

In 1649 the Puritans won. King Charles was deposed, and Cromwell came to power. But as soon as he was in power, Cromwell moved to suppress the radical Puritans who had helped bring him into power, in order to make a stronger alliance with those in England interested in economic expansion. Two groups of Cromwell's supporters were crushed. The Levellers, Puritans with a passion for reform, and the Diggers, even more radical advocates of economic change, were imprisoned, silenced, and punished.

The brokenhearted visionaries protested, demanding that the covenantal commitments be honored. Cromwell squelched their dissent. As a result, more Separatists came to America, placing their hope in a new land. Many remained in England, where new religious movements emerged. One was called the Ranters. The Ranters responded to the anguish of a broken covenant with frightening outbreaks of rage. In *The Covenant Crucified*, Quaker scholar Douglas Gywn likens the Ranters to the "unemployed ranks of punks in England of the 1970s snarling 'no future.'" They evolved a nihilistic theology that paired light and darkness as one and viewed good and evil as intertwined. When put in prison, they quickly recanted. Brokenhearted, they held to no principles that were worth living or dying for.

Another group to emerge was called the Seekers. Seekers were individuals who wandered from one group to another, seeking ways to repair the broken covenant. Unable to find any answers, they were united more by "their sense of what they had not found. But rather than lapse into nihilistic rage," Gwyn writes that the Seekers settled into a penitent silence that kept the covenant faith even beyond human understanding. . . . A renewed emphasis was placed upon the overwhelming power of God's grace and the need for human stillness to sense the spirit's motions. . . . They watched and waited in the dark night of eclipse.

One of these silent wanderers was George Fox, who was a youth when Cromwell turned on his coreligionists and dashed their hopes. Fox left home and traveled from village to village, asking the Puritan clergy if they could answer him in his suicidal despair. He sought refuge in nature, sleeping in open fields and in trees in the forest. For ten years he wandered, and in his wandering a new religious awareness came to him.

In the midst of the despair of the broken covenant, Fox began to experience the presence of a spirit sustaining him and all of life. He articulated this spiritual discovery with these words: "Inward life did spring up in me." From this spiritual discovery he formulated, in Gwyn's description "a deeper spiritual practice . . . a tender pacifism melded to a fierce commitment to social activism fueled by a sense of hope born through trial."

Among Unitarian Universalists, there is a deep spiritual longing. According to the Fulfilling the Promise Survey, over 75 percent of us feel something is missing in our faith. Asked to identify what is lacking, we name "spiritual discipline and depth." We need to see the longing for spirituality among us as an expression of our awareness of broken covenant, of something that is failing in our culture—a promise unfulfilled. All of us who have come into Unitarian Universalism from another religious context know something of promises broken. All human beings have experienced the impasse and anguish of violated trust.

We need to see our own longing for a deeper and more disciplined spiritual life as a sign that we know something is missing. But patient pursuit of what we need, even the willingness to wander without direction or relief, will bring fresh vision. The place of limit becomes the place of revelation.

The path to deeper spirituality begins in the experience of promises failed, covenant broken, hope suppressed. It begins with disillusionment, impasse, and grief, and it passes through the fire to a new revelation. In our time, seekers wander from church to church asking, "Can you answer my despair?" Ranters cry out in the public square, their anguish filling public space with the witness of our collective breach of faith. We suppress the seeker and the ranter—whether within us or around us—at our peril, for each is part of the path from broken covenant to a fresh discovery of the deeper resources for hope and strength. The pain of disappointment gives rise to new practices and new covenants that are strong enough to move us beyond the limits of our inheritance into fresh hope and creativity. Stillness that listens and rage that protests will guide us to a new covenant, if we have the courage to refuse to flee from our tears and to embody in everyday practices what we come to know.

We must continue to search until we find the illumination for our time. It came to George Fox alone in the wilderness, and it came to many of our religious ancestors in the community of resistance, the realization that we are part of a universal love. There is something that will not let us go. It is in obedience to this truth that the promise of life is fulfilled in us and we become a blessing to the world. We may come to know this love, as theologian Bill Jones describes it, as a fierce rebellion lodged in the human heart that will rage against oppression and injustice until the end. Or we may come to know it, as I have, as a divine comforter who has never left and will never leave, and who embraces even the violators of covenant with the fire of redeeming love. Regardless of how we come to this love, the experience of brokenness is the place of revelation, and that revelation is what will fuel a new covenant.

Given the lessons of history, I offer these possible expressions of our covenant: To keep faith with the source of life, knowing that we are not our own and that Earth made us; to keep faith with the community of resistance, never forgetting that life can be saved from that which threatens it by even small bands of people choosing to put into practice an alternative way of life; and to seek an ever deeper awareness of that which springs up inwardly in us. Even when our hearts are broken by our own failure or the failure of others, even when we have done all we can and life is still broken, there is a universal love that has never broken faith with us and never will.

This is the ground of our hope, and the reason that we can be bold in seeking to fulfill the promise.

Something Far More Deeply Interfused

I GREW UP IN A SMALL CORNER of southwest Washington in a town named Hoquiam, at the southern edge of the rain forest of the Olympic National Park. It's so rainy in Hoquiam that when I was a child, I believed summer was a one-day-a-year holiday, like Christmas. We had 160 inches of rain annually, and our whole world was wrapped in mist and moisture and gray skies.

My family had a hard time keeping body and soul together. We were rich in things of the spirit and poor in things of the flesh—which meant that when it came to summer vacations for that one-day holiday, we had to use all of our ingenuity to have as much fun as possible with scarce financial resources. So it became our family tradition to spend our summer vacations hiking the high country of the Olympic and the Cascade Mountains.

This was before the days when hiking had become the high-tech sport that it is today. All of our gear was makeshift. My very first backpack was something my father had constructed out of two halves of an old broomstick and a Girl Scout cookie box. We had a lot of fun making do with very little.

As teenagers, my two brothers, Howard and Theodore, and I used to go hiking by ourselves on occasion. One of our most memorable trips took us up to the high country of the Cascades, to a place where we'd never been: Spray Park Meadows, a high, alpine meadow on the shoulders of Mount Rainier. We began our hike at

Mowich Lake, under the protection of the tall forest. Like almost every hike we ever went on, this hike began in the rain. We wore our ponchos and our gators; we knew how to deal with the wet.

We hiked through the quiet, soft, drizzling rain for the first three-quarters of the day. Toward late afternoon, we found we were no longer hiking in the rain. We had walked right into a cloud. By the time we ascended through the forest up to the edges of the alpine meadow, the cloud encompassed us so thickly that we could only see the muddy trail ahead of us by staring straight down at our feet. Undaunted, we trudged across the meadow to the upper reaches where the heather was blooming and the Indian paintbrush was bending over, wet with dew.

We made a camp up against the edge of a high, protective boulder. We cooked our chicken soup, spread out our sleeping bags, and stretched our tarp. When all was set up, my brother Howard unfolded the geological survey map, studied it, and pronounced, "Mount Rainier must be around here somewhere!" We gathered around and stared at the compass. The arrow wavered unsteadily to the north, but even with an uncertain compass, we managed to figure out where we were. Howard traced our route. "Here's where we came, and here's where we must be right now, which means Mount Rainier must be right . . . there."

Now, this really happened. The instant Howard said, "Mount Rainer must be right . . . there," we all turned our heads and looked into the pea-soup fog. Just as we turned, the fog opened, like two opaque sliding glass doors pulling away from each other, and Mount Rainier was . . . there. Filling up the entire sky. It was just that moment of twilight when the sun was sinking over the Pacific Ocean, and the last long gleams of light were skimming across the snow-crested peaks of the Olympics. The upper edges of Mount Rainier were outlined with glints of gold, and the crevasses and valleys were deepening from magenta into purple into midnight blue. Behind the mountain the sky was turning into that shade of evening blue that cannot be named. The first stars were blinking forth. Wordsworth's poem "Lines Composed a Few

Miles Above Tintern Abbey" came to mind.

> And I have felt
> A presence that disturbs me with the joy
> Of elevated thoughts; a sense sublime
> Of something far more deeply interfused,
> Whose dwelling is the light of setting suns,
> And the round ocean and the living air,
> And the blue sky, and in the mind of man;
> A motion and a spirit, that impels
> All thinking things, all objects of all thought,
> And rolls through all things.

The hair on the back of my neck literally stood up. We held perfectly still, transfixed by this stunning beauty. And then the fog rolled back in on itself; the opaque sliding glass doors closed. We were wrapped once more in fine mist and couldn't see beyond our toes.

Our religious lives are like this. Most of the time we trudge through the lowland forest with makeshift packs on our backs. Our gear isn't quite what we need it to be. People look at what we're doing and say, "You're all wet!" Nevertheless, we keep on our path, continue going to meetings in our local congregations. We do what we can to study, learn, pray, worship, gather together with others, serve our communities, and make a difference. We stay with it. And then there are moments when we come to the upper edges of the alpine meadow, and the fog parts, and we find ourselves standing in the presence of a glory that transfixes us with its stunning beauty. We know that all along our labor and our work have been in relationship to this—this something far more deeply interfused. Always there, though rarely seen. In those moments we are strengthened in our commitments. Then the moment passes.

As religious liberals, we commit ourselves to principles, purposes, and ideals that are not mere abstractions. They are a conceptualization of the sacred land, a map drawn by those who have, themselves, stood in the presence of glory. With the map comes a promise: If you travel to this country, you will see great beauty.

Take, for example, the principle of tolerance, a fundamental premise of liberal religion. Most of us have reasons why we believe in tolerance. We understand the idea. For one thing, we have seen religious intolerance, and we don't want to see any more of it. We recognize how much conflict in the world is a consequence of refusing to see the contributions of our neighbors' religion as worthy of respect.

We think of Northern Ireland, the Middle East, India, and Pakistan, the struggles that have gone on for centuries in our own land between the imperial forms of Christianity and the native traditions that were present in pre-Columbian times. We agree with the Catholic theologian Hans Kung: There will be no peace in the world until there is peace among the world's religions.

An ancient Eastern teaching story illustrates the wisdom of tolerance: A group of blind people encounter an elephant, and each touches a different part. One touches the side of the elephant and says, "I know what this is. This is a wall." A second touches the leg of the elephant and says, "I know what this is. This is a tree." And another touches the tail and says, "I know what this is. This is a rope." Finally one of them touches the trunk and says, "This is a snake."

The point of this story is that each blind person has had a real encounter with the elephant, but no one of them alone has encountered the whole animal. The only way any one of them could know the whole truth would be if they each listened to what their neighbors knew. Believing in tolerance is more than just putting up with what our neighbor thinks; beyond that, we must recognize that our neighbor may know something vitally important about the ultimate mysteries of life that we, in our limited experience, have not even begun to imagine. And so, beyond tolerance, we practice openness to the one next to us, knowing that person may have something to contribute to us. Furthermore, we recognize that an individual search for the truth is not sufficient.

We must make a communal, collective, even global search for the ultimate values, mysteries, and meanings of life. And in that searching we are not isolated heroes, trying to comprehend the whole. Each one of us is a member of an expedition team with a neighbor who has something to teach us.

Some of us believe in tolerance because we have been persuaded by the post-Newtonian paradigm shift. Advances in physics suggest that it is naïve to think there is any point in the universe from which one has an absolute perspective on the whole. Every view of the truth is from a specific point on the space-time continuum. There is no perspective from above and beyond, only perspectives from within. And so, the whole looks different from every standpoint. We practice tolerance because the truth is always connected to a standpoint and a context.

No matter why we value it, the practice of tolerance leads us to experience other human beings in a new way. We begin to let go of all of our preset opinions and prejudices about the other. The fog that separates us begins to part, and the face of the other shines forth with its own authenticity. We begin to see each person's uniqueness. We don't define who they are; we allow them to define to us who they are. There's a name for this: love.

I learned something about this quality of love, which allows others to touch us, from a story that Elton Bennet, a local artist in my hometown used to tell, about what happened to him when Dorothy Smith moved to town. Dorothy was the most interesting woman that the men in Hoquiam had ever met. She graduated from Smith College, back east, and came to Hoquiam as a social worker. She was erudite, charming, and beautiful, and she liked to hike. What more could anyone in Hoquiam want? Elton decided to court Dorothy, but he wasn't the only one. So did Helgae Erikson.

Helgae was different from Elton. Helgae was not an artist but a logger. He was a very interesting man who not only logged the forest but was committed to the natural environment. He helped develop the Olympic National Park and built many of the trails. He was also an inventor and experimenter. I can remember as a small child going out to Helgae's cabin in the woods, where he was experimenting with generating electricity through the stream that went down by his house.

Helgae and Elton courted Dorothy at the same time. They both took her on long walks along Gray's Harbor River through the wet trees. While they walked, Elton sought to win Dorothy's heart by impressing her with his erudition; he talked to her about art and artists, poetry and politics, world events. He put on a marvelous display of how interesting he was.

Meanwhile, Helgae walked on the other side of Dorothy, and while they traipsed along the forest paths, Helgae held Dorothy's hand. Dorothy married Helgae, which proves that the pretense of our communication is not as important as those gestures and actions by which we become really present to one another. Tolerance makes such real hand-to-hand presence possible.

The second great principle of liberal religion is reason. Our liberal religious roots are in protest against a despairing and negative view of the human being. The nineteenth-century Universalists and Unitarians objected to the Calvinist doctrine of total depravity, which thought the human being was so wounded and fraught with sin at birth that a person could not be trusted to do what was right, comprehend what was just, or discern what was true. The only hope was to become obedient to sources of truth and revelation outside of one's self that were believed to possess a greater trustworthiness.

Authoritarian religion views human beings negatively and establishes sources of authority beyond human experience— sacred texts, holy leaders, or canonized tradition and law. These things have an authority that the individual cannot wield. A proper religious person submits obediently to external authority.

Our heritage rejects authoritarian religion and its negative view of human beings. Our forebears claimed a more positive view. They said we are born with capacities for good and evil and possess a whole array of gifts and abilities. Our powers can be used in the service of all sorts of values, but the choice is in our hands. Chief among the human gifts we celebrate is the capacity to think and to reason. Our affirmation of reason is part and parcel of our affirmation of the essential goodness and worthiness of human life. We replaced outside authorities with the inner authority of conscience and reason.

I learned about the importance of reason in religion from my grandmother Ernst, who was an old-fashioned, rationalist, liberal Christian. She taught that you should never believe anything unless you can, with your own mind, determine that it is trustworthy. My grandmother could dismiss whole systems of thought with one word: nonsense. Her ultimate criterion in theological and philosophical issues was, "Does it make sense?" Sense and nonsense—that was the dividing line for my grandmother.

My grandmother taught me about reason and religion the same way she taught me to hem a skirt. She had a radical theory of hemming skirts. She believed you should use a double thread and take the stitches so securely that they could be seen from the outside. The lesson is that you should never trust anything unless you, yourself, can see that it is stitched together well. And you should never give your trust to a system of thought unless you can understand its whole structure and test whether it is sturdy.

From my grandmother, I also learned the deeper importance of reason. Every day in the summer when I stayed with her at her Puget Sound cabin, we would go on the same three-quarter-mile trail through the woods. On that pathway we would stop every few feet as my grandmother taught me what I could observe with my senses. She'd say, "Listen. Do you hear that song? That's the meadowlark." She'd say, "Look through the trees there. Do you see that tall slender tree with the branches that come out evenly like this, with smooth bark? That's a Cascara tree, and from its bark you can make medicine that will heal the heart." She taught me the names of all the trees, all the shrubs, and all the wayside flowers on that one little three-quarter-mile trek. As the seasons changed, I learned when to look for the bloom of the skunk cabbage, when the gingerroot would come into full leaf, and when the colt's foot would be good to eat. Up and down that path I learned that reason is the practice of intimate attention to the world. In that intimate attention, fog falls away. The earth itself becomes more and more vivid as a real presence. It becomes full of faces, each with its own character and uniqueness. The world buzzes with living presences, and the intrinsic value of things becomes clear. The practice of reason comes down to an experience of the real presence of the earth; it comes down to love.

Along with tolerance and reason, liberal religion is characterized by freedom. We believe in freedom because we believe in the sacred worth of every individual human being. We do not want the potential of any human being to be constrained by inability to participate in decision making (democracy), lack of the fundamentals needed for survival (food, shelter, health care), or by insufficient access to those things that nurture the full growth of our spirits (freedom of religion, education). We work hard in countless ways to ensure and protect human freedom because we want to see the full flourishing of every human being. We don't want to see the soul and spirit imprisoned or cut off. We rejoice when totalitarian systems fall and make room for fresh opportunities.

Sometimes that which constrains us is within our own being. Some of us are in bondage to deep wounds from which we have been unable to heal. Others are imprisoned by an internalized message that we have nothing to offer, that our gifts or talents are worth nothing. Sometimes the internal oppressor keeps us from ever doing that which we are most capable of doing or contributing our gifts to the larger human family. The internal oppressor can keep us from showing our own true face to the people we love most. Our liberal religious commitment to freedom includes the challenge of finding our own freedom.

Early in my ministry, I caught a glimpse of what we might call "spiritual freedom," and simultaneously, of how much I lacked that freedom. I was one of those young people who went straight from college to seminary to the parish. At twenty-four, I found myself the minister of a small congregation—very small, fortunately. My first few years in ministry were difficult, as I think they are for most beginning ministers of any age. I struggled constantly with my feeling that I could never meet everybody's expectations. Everybody had different things that they wanted me to be good at or wanted me to do. I used to lie awake at night, worrying that I couldn't meet these expectations. It hadn't occurred to me that I didn't need to meet all the expectations. I was sure I was supposed to.

I was also overwhelmed at the astonishing depth of suffering among the people I was called to serve and how hidden from others that suffering often was. The people in my church had buried aspects of themselves. They carried sorrows and pains that they kept secret from each other and told only the minister. I had to confront the realities of people who were severely beaten throughout their childhoods and people who were sexually abused. I hadn't known that men come home from war with haunting scars. I hadn't known that adults sometimes lose their children to death. And I was overwhelmed by feeling that I had no resources for adequately responding to the needs of the people around me. I thought, "I have nothing to give." Then I really couldn't sleep at night!

All of this difficulty came to a crisis one Friday afternoon. All week, there had been so many pastoral emergencies that the church bulletin wasn't ready yet for Sunday morning. Just as I was frantically trying to finish choosing the readings for Sunday, the phone rang. It was the husband of a young woman in the church. He was calling from the hospital. He said, "Debbie has gone into labor." I knew that the child wasn't due for another six weeks. "They've told us that the baby is dead. Will you come?"

I hung up the phone and turned to Dorris, the church secretary, who had been assisting the minister for forty years. "Dorris, Debbie is in labor, and the child is going to be stillborn. What shall I do? What can I do? I don't know what to say to her. How is she going to go through this whole pain of labor knowing that she's not laboring to give birth to life?"

Dorris looked at me and said, "Do what the angels do."

But I didn't believe in angels. I flashed back to my grandmother telling me I shouldn't believe anything unless I could see how it was stitched together. But I was desperate. So I asked, "What do the angels do?" And Dorris answered, "Just be there."

I went to the hospital, and I remember crossing the threshold into the room where Debbie was sweating and struggling in labor. When I entered the room, she looked at me in her exhaustion and stretched out her hand. I walked over to the bedside and put my hand into hers. She gripped mine very tightly. I didn't have any words to say. But at that moment, I felt like the mountain. I was there. It was enough. And that's when I learned, or glimpsed, that freedom is being present, being there, not performing, not saving or changing the world necessarily, but being there. In the moments we are doing that, we are free. The practice of freedom is like tolerance and reason; it comes down to love.

Liberal religion is not a head trip. Its values and principles are not something dreamed up by armchair philosophers who think these might be good things to believe. The principles of tolerance and reason and freedom are principles articulated by those who have touched and been touched by life. To be committed to these principles is to follow a path that leads us into deep intimacy with those things of abiding beauty and power that are holy, a path that leads us to love. And so I suggest that the purpose of our religious life is to see the mountain; and when we can't see the mountain, to feel the mountain; and when we can't feel the mountain, to be the mountain. And if there are moments when we can neither see, nor feel, nor be the mountain, then read the map.

On This Shining Night

On occasion i have said that my career goal is to be tried for heresy. The closest I've come so far happened when I participated with a group of feminist theologians in the publication of *Christianity, Patriarchy, and Abuse.* In this book, Rita Nakashima Brock, Marie Fortune, Carter Heyward, Beverly Harrison, Joanne Brown, a few others, and I presented a contemporary feminist critique of the doctrine on which the Universalist Hosea Ballou centered his attention 185 years ago, the substitutionary theory of atonement.

Ballou rejected the idea of atonement, and we followed suit. Our concern, however, was different from his. Ballou criticized the doctrine of atonement because he believed it didn't make sense under the light of reason. It was logically inconsistent to imagine a loving God who would require brutal punishment as payment for sin.

We believed the doctrine didn't make sense in light of experiences of physical abuse. We were concerned with violations of the body. We argued that when God is imagined to save the world by requiring that his beloved child die, human beings tend to identify with the requirements placed on that divine child. People come to believe their violation is divinely required, and they regard their suffering as virtuous and redemptive.

As feminist theologians, we reflected on our pastoral experience with battered women. We knew women who had stayed in abusive relationships because ministers and priests had told them that being battered made them Christ-like. We knew adult survivors of childhood abuse who believed as children that their silence in the face of their suffering was good behavior. They were like Jesus, a silent lamb led to the slaughter. There are parallels to the experiences of abused women and children in the experiences of soldiers in war. Soldiers are required to sacrifice themselves to give life to abstract values greater than themselves: democracy, freedom, or the fatherland. In war, a teenage boy is asked, like the son of God, to give his life in obedience to his father—a military father, a presidential father, a sovereign father—who requires his death to redeem the world.

When we published our critique of the doctrine of atonement, declaring that the death of Jesus on the cross did not save anyone, I could feel the possibility of being tried for heresy coming close. My co-writer Joanne Brown, who was teaching theology at Pacific Lutheran University, came under immediate attack. The administration of the university moved to fire her. In a Lutheran university, even in 1989, to say that the death of Jesus on the cross did not redeem the world was to preach and teach heresy.

When this happened to Joanne, I went to see my eighty-three-year-old grandmother, Katherine Ernst. She read our article and talked with me about our experience. "What is all this fuss about?" she asked, astonished. "We did away with the doctrine of the atonement a long time ago. A loving God doesn't need a bloody sacrifice to forgive us. People who make the death and resurrection of Jesus the center of their religion are all wrapped up in a myth. They make a myth their religion so they can avoid following the teachings of Jesus."

She went on, "Do you want to know how I believe we are saved? I believe we are saved by those human beings in every time and place who have stayed faithful to the truth in spite of threat."

My hopes for a heresy trial faded when I recognized my grandmother's radicalism was way beyond mine.

News of Joanne's threatened firing reached her colleagues in the religion department of Pacific Lutheran University. They were alarmed. Though all of them were deeply troubled by Joanne's position and considered it heresy, their Lutheran faith held that God works through human minds and hearts. They knew from their religious tradition that the Spirit sometimes breaks through in fresh thinking, shattering established dogma. Even a pope might turn out to be the Antichrist! One could not fetter free thinking without fettering God.

The religion faculty—all conservative white men—joined together and announced that they would all resign if Joanne were fired. The administration backed off, Joanne's job was saved, and in this remarkable way, orthodox Lutheran scholars who couldn't disagree more proved my radical grandmother's theory of salvation. They risked their own economic well-being to stand for what they knew: Freedom of thought must be protected to preserve room for the workings of the spirit.

When I made a commitment to the Unitarian Universalist movement, I thought, "This is not the religious group to affiliate with if you want to be tried for heresy." But I was cheered to discover in the study of Universalist history that there was at least one heresy trial.

Herman Bisbee was charged with heretical preaching in 1872. Influenced by Emerson's notions of natural religion, Bisbee emphasized the primacy of reason over revelation. He was interested in non-Christian religious ideas and placed his trust in the perfectibility of human beings. His colleagues accused him of bringing unhealthy Unitarian influences into Universalism. Universalist leaders, anxious to solidify their cause, had been advocating greater unity. The 1870 Centennial Conference reaffirmed the Winchester Profession without the liberty clause that had supported freedom of conscience. The 1871 Conference declared, "the Universalist Denomination will move in concert, and as one grand and well-disciplined army, in the warfare to which it is appointed among the spiritual forces of this world."

The climate for a heresy trial was created by enthusiasm for unity. Bisbee ventured unorthodox ideas and was met with censure.

Even with the climate ripe for creedal conflicts, one must ask what Universalists, traditionally open-minded, generous-hearted, inclusive people, would find to be beyond the pale. What do you have to say to raise the orthodox eyebrows of a Universalist?

The charges against Bisbee were based in part on his sermon of March 27, 1870. He said, "In natural religion there is no gift. Salvation does not come by grace." Perhaps this is the essence of heresy for a Universalist, the denial of grace. Perhaps this denial still troubles the relationship of Universalism and Unitarianism.

Universalist interpretations of universal salvation are varied. But I believe all of them can be read as an effort to give expression to a deep religious intuition that all of our lives are unquestionably grounded in grace. There is a gift that is given to all people and embraces the whole of creation, a gift that does not have to be earned, that will never be lost, and that cannot be taken away.

Consider John Murray's theology. His gospel may ring foreign to our ears now, but it is a theology of radical grace. He preached that through the death of Jesus on the cross, all of humanity was redeemed, once and for all. Because of his belief that this redemptive act included all people, he rejected the Calvinist notion that only some are saved. Salvation is for all and embraces all. To people who were living with the oppressive fear that they might be outside the circle of God's redeeming action, Murray proclaimed the good news that all were within the circle of grace.

The power of this gospel was its proclamation that the gift has already been given. What we hope for has already happened. We are already standing in the promised land. We are already loved. We are already healed. All of us. In the power of this message of grace, we can live free from fear.

In his *Treatise on Atonement*, Hosea Ballou departs from Murray. He does not believe that the death of Jesus on the cross was the literal sacrifice that freed all from sin. Ballou found that view in conflict with his belief in a loving God. He goes on, however, to proclaim that we are saved by the universal love of God. The spirit of God's love is already present in all of life, and grounded in that love, we are invited by Ballou's theology to live in a way that affirms this gift.

A Universalist ethic unfolds from this theology: Since all are loved by God, we are called to love all, to devote our lives to justice, mercy, and compassion. Ballou, furthermore, believed that the final happiness and holiness of all creation would evolve through the workings of love present now in the world. He was confident in love's final triumph over everything that degrades and harms life.

If we look to later Universalism, from Mary Livermore to Clarence Skinner, we see this hope develop in theology and in committed lives. Universalists acted on their belief that through the love of God working in the world, the world would eventually be wholly transformed into the Kingdom of God.

Skinner found a compatible vision in the Social Gospel movement that arose in the late nineteenth century and continued to define much of liberal Protestantism in America into the 1940s and 1950s, culminating in the life and thought of Martin Luther King Jr. and the movement he inspired.

With Clarence Skinner, Universalism continued to claim the prophetic hope of ancient Israel. The time will come when the whole creation is restored. No one will be hungry or homeless. The scarred earth will become an abundant garden. Tears will be wiped from every eye, all children will be loved, war will cease, and suffering will come to an end. The kingdom of God was the image of hope at the center of Skinner's theology. There is a mystical dimension to this hope. In Skinner, we see such a deep confidence that this kingdom will arrive that it is as if the kingdom of God is already here.

Gordon McKeeman, a former president of the Starr King School for the Ministry, gave me my first grasp of Universalism in this spirit. When I asked what Universalists believed, he said, "Universalists believe that all of us are going to end up together in heaven, so we might as well learn how to get along with each other now."

McKeeman's summary captures the power of prophetic imagination. If we imagine a world in which there is peace, justice, and love for all, where the divisions that tear us apart are eliminated—and if we have a deep, confident faith that this will come into being—then we live from the perspective of ultimate hope, what theologians call "realized eschatology." We imagine what can be, and we make our lives a realization of that hope. We live with serenity and courage. We live confident that one can exist without fear, centered in love, and motivated by what Skinner called "radiant hope."

Universalism has had a fragile presence in the world. A student of Universalist history will note how much soul-searching has been given over to the question of why Universalism hasn't held its ground. Sometimes institutional failures are blamed, or a lack of energy. At one point, some Universalists argued that their work was done; the mission had been accomplished, and there was no longer a need for an organized Universalist denomination.

I would like to offer a theological perspective on the fragility of Universalism's place in the world. It is difficult to trust, sustain, or pass on the faith that "grace happens," that there is a gift already given to us all that is absolutely trustworthy and irrevocable. Universalism is fragile because its faith is fragile.

From the perspective of the late twentieth century, the fragility of this faith is particularly vivid to me. If we take an honest look at our history, our world, and ourselves, we have to admit that trust in a grace that upholds us all is not at the core of most of our beings. I believe we profoundly doubt grace.

We doubt it as liberals. Here I speak from my own experience as a person shaped by the tradition of liberal, social gospel Christianity. I was raised believing, like Skinner, that the Kingdom of God will be realized on earth. But where Skinner holds to radiant hope, I'm afraid we liberal Methodists were just into hard work. God's Kingdom will come, but we have to build it.

Liberal theology has focused in strong and positive ways on

our capacities to bring in the kingdom of God. We can make it. We can build it. The magazine *The Christian Century* was founded at the beginning of the twentieth century in the belief that the time had come when the whole world would be transformed into the hoped-for realm of God.

For many of us, the confidence that we ourselves can build heaven on earth has been the essence of liberating faith. We recognize that we are not just pawns of fate; that everything is not predetermined by God; that we are the agents of history, we are the creators. We have the freedom to do, and to choose, and to make.

This positive, proactive faith has held us committed to liberal religion. We celebrate our hope in ourselves in a world where religious movements continue to disempower human beings. Authoritarian and life-suppressing religious traditions survive and even dominate our culture. They teach us that passivity is a virtue, that God will take care of everything, that the future is already fated. We are required to grasp again and again the confidence of our faith that we have power, authority, and strength.

But our will-centered religion comes to a crisis. We discover that the world does not appear to be any better off after two hundred years of social activism. We despair. On a personal level, many of us come to a life crisis that forces us to face the fact that there is something broken in this world—in ourselves, our families, our churches, our workplaces, our communities—that for all our ingenuity, commitment, and genius, we cannot fix. We come up against our helplessness, the inability to stop loved ones from dying, or turn our children from paths of self-destruction, or keep riots from happening. Sometimes we can't even get our own churches to be places where people are civil to one another. We come up against the limits of our faith. We may find ourselves asking, "Is there any source of help beyond my own strength? Is there anything I can trust beyond our power to make it right? Or must I hope just in this: that if we work hard enough, maybe things will be okay?" That's a hope tinged with tremendous sadness and tiredness, and it is very difficult to sustain.

The faith of Universalism is fragile because it is continually assaulted by life experiences that teach us to doubt. Our own life experiences of tragedy or violence, as well as our awareness of what happened in the twentieth century and what is happening now, force us to confront a magnitude of evil that makes it hard to trust that we are saved. The most obvious thing is not that we are saved; the most obvious thing is that the world is full of brokenness, suffering, and injustice. Even our own lives, our own hearts and bodies, are fraught with pain.

After Auschwitz, the congenial assurance of Ballou that the loving spirit will bring about happiness and holiness for all seems naïve. Mary Livermore's triumphant confidence in the dawn of a new age seems inflated, even irrational. We agree with Woody Allen: "If there is a God, clearly this God is an underachiever."

Faith, as the old Universalists understood it, involves a form of trust that we in our century have lost. This loss of faith cannot be fully understood without recognizing that it stems in part from the larger historical movement that has shaped our culture in the West, the Enlightenment. The Enlightenment tradition conditions us to doubt. When Descartes came to the conclusion, "I think, therefore I am," he marked the loss of the sensibility "I feel, therefore I am," "I taste the oranges, therefore I am," "My hand touches yours and I feel joy, therefore I am."

The Enlightenment tradition, as represented by Descartes, elevates mind over body to such an extent that it raises doubt regarding the body's significance, or even existence. We cannot know the world exists; we can only know that our mental operations exist. We cannot know there is any objective reality; we can only know our subjective experience. The world becomes nothing more than a projection of the mind.

This development in philosophy and culture has significant implications for faith. Faith becomes a subjective stance; nothing can be given to us from a source beyond ourselves. How can I really know that you exist? All I really know is that I imagine you. If I don't even know, confidently, that you are here, or that the world is here, how will I ever be able to trust that there is something that will assist me in my suffering?

To doubt the existence of the world is implicitly to doubt grace. The sweet smell of a rose is not a gift but a projection. Nothing was given to us, no cup of water, no sunset, no Beethoven symphony. We dreamed it all up.

Doubt this profound leads to senseless violence. Under the influence of the alienated, "enlightened" mind, it's easy to bomb Baghdad because we fail to imagine the reality of other people's lives, cultures, and histories. It's easy to violate the environment, cut down the rain forests, and practice agriculture in a way that makes the earth barren. With an alienated mind, care becomes impossible.

Care for the world is closely linked to the understanding that life is a gift. Once that link is severed, neither grace nor justice has a chance. The Universalists have been right to link an ethic of responsibility with a doctrine of universal salvation. The doctrine affirms grace, and the ethic lives it. When trust in grace is lost, an ethic of responsibility becomes a matter of willpower alone and cannot be sustained.

In a crisis, we discover that facing the depth of tragedy straight on brings us to a place where we can hardly bear to live without hope. We have all probably had at least one time in life when we came to that depth of despair, when we pondered the deepest question that I believe all religion must address: Am I willing to live?

I asked that question once.

It had been a year of grief. In a situation of broken love, I chose to have an abortion. I felt it was the only thing I could do, but I was haunted by the loss of that surrendered child. My grief deepened as days passed. Time was not healing my sorrow, and I spiraled into deeper and deeper despair. By day I would dutifully, and to all appearances cheerfully, perform my responsibilities as the minister of a small and vibrant congregation. At night, I couldn't sleep. I'd rise, pace the empty halls of the parsonage, and wail.

My despair and isolation came to a crisis one night. I was past living one day at a time, or even one hour at a time, and was down to the question of whether I would be willing to continue to live at all. In the depths of that sadness, I decided to stop pacing the hall. It was after midnight. I left my house and walked down the hill to Lake Union. The city was quiet. My face was wet with tears as I set my course toward the water's edge. I was determined to walk into the lake's cold darkness and find there the consolation that I could not find within myself.

At the bottom of the hill, the street ended and the lakeside park began. I walked across the wet grass and climbed the last rise before the final descent to the water's edge. As I crested the rise, I discovered a line of dark objects between me and the shore, a barricade I was going to have to cross to get to the water.

I didn't remember this barricade being there before, and it was so dark that I couldn't tell what I was seeing. But as I edged closer, I discovered it was a line of human beings, hunched over some strange-looking, spindly equipment. Telescopes.

It was the Seattle Astronomy Club.

There they were with their homemade Heathkit telescopes and their top-of-the-line Sharper Image telescopes, dressed in their Gore-Tex back-country gear and tennis shoes. A whole club of amateur scientists, up and alert in the middle of the night because the sky was clear and the planets were near.

To make my way to my death, I had to get past an enthusiast in tennis shoes. He assumed I had come to look at the stars. "Here. Let me show you," he said, and began to explain the star cluster his telescope was focused on. I had to brush the tears from my eyes to look through his telescope. There it was! A red-orange spiral galaxy. Then he focused it on Jupiter, and I peered through to see the giant, glowing planet. I could not bring myself to continue my journey. In a world where people get up in the middle of the night to look at the stars, I could not end my life.

I know there is grace, because my life was saved by the Seattle Astronomy Club.

When I think about that experience, I realize it holds many clues about how to trust grace. What saved me in that moment is difficult to fully name. That night, I was saved by people who held fast to their desire to see the beauty of the universe, in spite of the cold or the late hour. No threats, I'm sure, would have kept those enthusiasts from looking at the stars. I was saved by the human capacity to love the world and the distant reaches of the unknown. I was saved by one particular human being who assumed I shared a desire to see the stars. I was saved by being met, right in the center of the pathway of my despair, by one—actually one hundred—who wouldn't let me go that way. I was saved by the stars themselves, by the cool green grass under my feet, by the earth, the cosmos, its presence, which won me over and persuaded me to stay.

I believe that we must doubt our doubt that there is grace. We must open ourselves to the possibility that there are sources beyond ourselves that sustain us, transform us, save us, that hold us tight in the arms of life. I believe that we must open ourselves to the possibility that this grace is already here, that it has been given, is being given, and will be given.

On reflection, I can see that throughout my life I have been tried for heresy—the heresy of believing that there is no gift. Life tries every one of us for this heresy. And in the trial we find ourselves having to face the truth: There is grace. We have to witness that, in fact, we are helped by love, by the earth, by the stars, and by that spirit inside of us that is moved by beauty or curiosity or surprise, when we thought life was not worth living.

My grandmother believed that we are saved by those who came before us, who held fast to the truth in spite of threat: John Murray and Hosea Ballou and Mary Livermore and Olympia Brown and Clarence Skinner and all those who have witnessed to the confident trust that there is a gift that is never taken away. These are our saviors.

We have to choose whom we will trust in this life. Let us trust those who believed. Let us join their company, keep faith with them, become part of the astronomy club, the choir, the congregation, the front lines. When we do so, it becomes tangible that heaven is here, and we are sustained in our work for justice by the depth of our trust—not our fear, or grief, or will—but our trust, our unshakeable confidence. It is as James Agee says, "Sure, on this shining night I weep for wonder."

Family Values

WHEN I WAS A SMALL CHILD, I came home from vacation Bible school one June singing:

> Jesus loves me this I know,
> For the Bible tells me so.
> Little ones to him belong,
> They are weak and he is strong.

My mother stopped my singing. I got the distinct impression she would prefer that I never sing that song again. When I became an adult, I asked my mother—who is, after all, the daughter and wife of Methodist ministers—what her objection was. She said, "I didn't think children should be taught to believe something just because the Bible said so. They should form their own religious thoughts from their experiences. Children shouldn't be told that they are weak; they need to discover their capacities and strengths.

"I suppose," she continued, "I didn't like you singing 'Jesus Loves Me' because it contradicted everything I was trying to accomplish as a parent. I wasn't trying to teach you to be obedient to my rules or anyone else's, and I didn't want you to think you were helpless. I wanted to help you become responsible to yourself and grounded in your strengths."

The fact that my mother—and my father as well—approached child-rearing as the nurturing of their children's gifts was a good fortune that blessed my life. But their family values did not emerge from nowhere. As Christian humanists, my parents operated from a framework of values that had taken 150 years to take root in mainline Protestant culture —a framework that was strongly represented not only in their church but in the public schools, which followed the educational philosophy of religious humanist John Dewey.

The family values of liberal theology originated in the earliest critique of Christian orthodoxy. This critique goes back at least as far as early nineteenth-century Universalists like Hosea Ballou. Ballou rejected the image of God as a cruel father who would be pleased by nothing more than the suffering death of his son Jesus on the cross. In his 1805 *Treatise on Atonement*, he writes,

> The belief that the great Jehovah was offended with his creatures to that degree, that nothing but the death of Christ, or the endless misery of mankind, could appease his anger, is an idea that has done more injury to the Christian religion than the writings of all its opposers, for many centuries. The error has been fatal to the life and spirit of the religion of Christ in our world; all those principles which are to be dreaded by men have been believed to exist in God; and professors have been molded into the image of their Deity, and become more cruel.

Ballou understood that how people imagine God influences the social structures they create and how they, themselves, behave. Theology and family values are inextricably linked: If God is a strict father who demands punishment for human sin, earthly fathers should follow suit.

As liberals, we have not only critiqued but also reframed theology into a different image of family, a different practice of love, and a different social agenda—with all three of these intertwined.

In place of a punishing father-God, nineteenth-century religious liberals reimagined God as a gentle, nurturing parent. Using the gender stereotypes of the time, this took them beyond "God the Father." In his autobiographical "Experience as a Minister," Theodore Parker writes, "I have called God Father, but also Mother . . . to express more sensibly the quality of tender and unselfish love, which mankind associates more with Mother."

Nineteenth- and early twentieth-century feminists keenly understood the relationship between their political hopes and the power of religion, and they began to reframe fundamental religious issues. Universalist reformer and writer Charlotte Perkins Gilman wrote *His Religion and Hers* in 1923. She says,

> Birth-based religion would steadily hold before our eyes the vision of a splendid race . . . the duty of upbuilding it. To the mother comes the apprehension of God as something coming; she sees his work, the newborn child, as visibly unfinished and calling for continuous service. . . . As the thought of God slowly unfolded in the mind of woman, that great Power would have been apprehended as the Life-giver, the Teacher, the Provider, the Protector—not the proud, angry, jealous, vengeful deity men have imagined.

Liberal and feminist theologians did more than reframe the God metaphors; they also reimagined humanity. Unitarian William Ellery Channing rejected Calvinism's picture of human beings as depraved sinners, incapable of doing God's will without God's all-powerful help. Instead, Channing said each one of us is born good, filled with a marvelous array of gifts and capacities. Channing called these "powers of the soul" the impress of divinity on our own nature. The purpose of life, religion, and education, Channing said, is to unfold and direct aright all the powers of the soul and thus to grow in our likeness to God.

By reframing old theological "family values," Unitarians and Universalists set social revolutions into motion. Family values that imagined God as a nurturing parent and humanity as gifted and sacred brought moral pressure to bear on the institution of slavery. Channing's theology inspired his parishioner Margaret Fuller to advocate for women's opportunities to grow their souls—as thinkers, artists, political activists, and educators. It inspired his parishioner Elizabeth Peabody to establish a kindergarten movement in the United States, introducing a new, humanistic vision that children, given an environment of nurture, respect, and guided stimulation, would unfold like seeds planted in good soil. Channing's positive image of the human soul also motivated Horace Mann to lead the movement that established free public education in the United States. Why free public education? Because all children—not just the children of the wealthy—should have the chance to discover their strengths and grow their souls. The twentieth-century educators John Dewey and Sophia Fahs built on these progressive religious values as they developed their educational philosophy and practice. This reframing fueled movements for peace, from Julia Ward Howe's first Mother's Day Proclamation, to Dr. Spock's opposition to the Vietnam War, to present-day Unitarian Universalists protesting the war in Iraq. These and many other concerns are not just political issues for us; they are religious issues because our family values are concerned with the sacred worth of all souls.

I became vividly aware that the old framework of family values was beginning to reassert itself in American culture in the mid-1980s. The occasion was a Vacation Bible School planning meeting among the Methodists, Lutherans, Presbyterians, and Baptists in my neighborhood. One woman came to the meeting full of enthusiasm for a curriculum produced by James Dobson and his conservative religious organization, Focus on the Family. The committee members dutifully took the sample materials home to review. I read the parent's guide. It began by explaining that children are marred by original sin from birth. You could see clear evidence of this, Dobson said, in children's rebellious spirits and disobedience. Christian parents had an obligation to lead their children to salvation, which began with discipline that rewarded good behavior and punished bad behavior. The Christian parent would not hesitate to use the paddle or the switch when necessary to make the child fear the parent enough to obey. This would prepare them for appropriate fear of the Lord. Vacation Bible School would help with all of this. It was "Jesus Loves Me" on steroids.

At the next committee meeting, the proposal that we use this curriculum was successfully defeated, but I didn't forget the name of James Dobson or Focus on the Family. Dobson's powerful organization has mobilized voters around issues like abortion and homosexuality—each of which is explicitly denounced as the failure of good fathering. His website includes advice on whether it is better to spank with your bare hand or to use a paddle or switch. It tells parents that they can prevent homosexuality by teaching children traditional gender roles and punishing gender-inappropriate behavior. Without strict guidance, boys won't grow up to be men who know how to discipline and protect their children and "respect" women, and girls won't grow up to be women who know how to focus on the needs of their husband and children, in loving submission. In kindly and reasoned prose, with quotes from people with doctorates in various fields, it explains that the best way to protect your family and bring your children up right is to accept Jesus as your personal Lord and Savior who died for your sins.

Historically, the theological notion that Jesus died on the cross in order to atone for human sin re-framed state violence into a story of family values. Imperial Rome, which had used crucifixion to terrorize and control subjugated people, was replaced as the agent of violence by God the Father, who required the crucifixion of his son. This twist turned the historical reality of imperial, political violence into a *Father Knows Best* episode, with the son as the exemplar of loving obedience, even unto death. This theology fueled the first Crusade and marks the turn of Christianity toward holy war. It was culturally propagated through the production of images of the tortured son of God twisting on the cross—images that had never been seen during the first thousand years of Christianity. No wonder that in 2004, cadets at the Air Force Academy in Colorado Springs were pressured to see Mel Gibson's film *The Passion of the Christ*.

The themes of the crucifixion story unite love with violence, fatherhood with holy war, and filial duty with the willingness to kill or be killed. At the same time, this theological history is linked to economic patterns of colonization that offer the poor hope only through military service that assists the wealthy to gain more control of territories and resources.

This theology is not Christianity's only form, but this is the form of Christianity that is dominating current politics and reshaping the character of our nation. It is a theology that, above all, functions to sanction violence and mask the face of imperialism. When it is deeply inscribed on the soul and hardwired into the brain, it curtails ethical reasoning that questions obedience to unjust commands.

The linguist George Lakoff has demonstrated how politics in the United States is shaped by the metaphor of the nation as family. The strict father framework, he argues, leads to cutbacks in social welfare systems. It seeks to stop handouts to the "undeserving." It promotes policies that justify preemptive war and sees punishment and retribution as keys to justice making. On the other hand, the nurturing parent framework of religious liberalism engenders social policies that care for the disadvantaged and vulnerable, promote international cooperation on behalf of a more just and peaceful world, and seek justice that repairs harm and restores right relationship. Theology matters. The time for religious progressives to reclaim the public square and reassert our family values is now.

One Fourth of July weekend, my family gathered for the fifty-first Parker family picnic at my parents' home on the Puget Sound. In many ways, we are an ordinary American family. We are racially and culturally diverse; our ancestral roots are in Alaska, Ireland, France, Switzerland, Korea, China, Hawaii, and more. Some of us are straight, and some of us are queer. One of us is an executive for a multinational corporation, and another is an antitrust attorney who breaks up monopolies. We count among us a still shell-shocked veteran of the Battle of the Bulge, as well as several life-long war resisters. Some of us are Jews, some Unitarian Universalists, some Christians. That weekend, we ate our water-melon, barbecued our chicken, and cranked the ice cream freezer. At twilight, as the evening stars came out and the water turned to a black mirror, we set fireworks off into the night sky. At the conclusion of the glittering display, we gathered around the campfire. Sparklers were handed out, and my mother—the one who wouldn't let us sing "Jesus Loves Me"—told us it was time to sing. She ruled out "The Star Spangled Banner" with its image of bursting bombs as the basis for patriotic joy. Instead, she passed out the words to one of her favorite hymns. Holding our sparklers aloft, we raised our voices to sing our family values.

Not alone for mighty empires
Stretching over land and sea
Not for battle ship and fortress
Sing we, God, our praise to thee

But for triumphs of the spirit
For the home, the church, the school
For the call to love our neighbor
In a land the people rule.

This is our country. Let us love it for all we are worth and do everything in our power to save its soul from the follies of bad theology.

BLESSING THE WORLD

WHAT SHALL WE DO
WITH ALL THIS BEAUTY?

AT THE END OF HIS EXTRAORDINARY ESSAY, "The Fire Next Time," James Baldwin poses a question. Most of the essay is a keen and painful exposition of the depth of loss and grief people of African descent experience in North American culture. Drawing on his experiences growing up in the ghettos of New York City, Baldwin shows us how self-loathing grows in a culture that tells a black child his presence is not welcome. He reveals how a sense of the sacredness of other human beings is lost, how relationship is severed, how ugliness permeates all aspects of living, and how despair closes down over people's lives.

But at the end of the essay, Baldwin invokes the rhythms of jazz, the resilience of spirit, the freshness of new life embodied in children growing up in the community, and he says, "The question remains: What do we do with all this beauty?" The greatest challenge in our lives is the challenge presented to us by the beauty of life, by what beauty asks of us, and by what we must do to keep faith with the beauty that has nourished our lives.

This question is important because we are living in an ugly time. I will not recite the litany of oppression, injustice, and environmental degradation because it is all too familiar, repeated before our eyes every day as we read the newspaper and watch the news. But to make matters worse, in the midst of this ugliness comes an ugly analysis. Some on the Right blame the rise of violence, the disruption of our sense of common life together, and the feeling of lost values on the movements arising from the world's oppressed. Social crisis, they claim, is caused by women who want equality; people of color who demand opportunities for education and employment; lesbian, gay, bisexual, and transgender people who want to live with honesty and as fully participating citizens; young, poor women who have so little hope or opportunity for their lives that the best they long for is a child to hold in their arms; artists who too blatantly hold up a mirror to us; youth who dramatically act out the greed and selfishness that we teach them; and of course the bleeding-heart liberals who tolerate them all.

This ugly analysis says the cure for America's sickness of soul is to lock up more criminals, make the poor fend for themselves, shut the doors to immigrants, remove the social safety net, roll back women's rights, and silence the arts. This analysis has undergirded conservative social policy since Newt Gingrich's 1994 "Contract with America." I once heard Jim Forbes, the minister of Riverside Church in New York City, say, "Someone has forged God's signature on the Contract with America." The Right's analysis is bad social policy and bad religion. It is an inadequate analysis of what ails our country and a dangerous prescription for how to heal the nation's soul. No nation was ever healed by shutting the door on those whose presence it fears. Such action on a national level was the source of the greatest tragedies in the twentieth century—Stalin's purges, Hitler's gas chambers, Pol Phot's killing fields. If we think our nation is above such atrocities, then our eyes are not open enough, our memories not long enough, and our thinking not alert enough.

The times we live in demand something of us. In fact, I believe they demand more from us than many of us ever expected. One of my friends says, "Everyone likes to have the best asked of them." I believe that we are living in a time when the best is asked of us, and this best is far beyond what we thought we were capable of or what we thought we would ever be asked to do. I believe that in rising to the occasion of what is asked of us now, we will discover a depth of strength and a richness of love and courage that we did not know we could claim or achieve. I believe that in rising to the challenge of our times we will wade into the mystery of life to a depth we did not know was available to us.

How shall we meet this challenge?

First of all, our times demand that we exercise our capacity for prophetic witness. By prophetic witness, I mean our ability to see what is happening, to say what is happening, and to ensure that our actions—personal and collective—accord with what we know. In another famous passage from "The Fire Next Time," Baldwin writes, "This is the crime of which I accuse my countrymen, for which I and history will never forgive them: that they have destroyed and are destroying hundreds and thousands of lives and do not know it and do not want to know it." A prophet is one who is able to name those places in our lives where we are resisting what needs to be known, closing our eyes to what is really happening, silencing what the world is telling us. Silence and denial create an environment in which violence and evil flourish.

But to see what is happening, to say what is happening, and then to act in accordance with what we know is no simple task. It often means breaking through our own silences and numbness. Spiritual activist and teacher Joanna Macy teaches a course called "Despair and Empowerment." After many years of social justice work, particularly on behalf of the environment, Joanna came to the conviction that the primary barrier that prevents us from doing what is necessary to save the planet is our inability to face the realities of our world.

We can watch the images flicker on our television screens, but to know what is happening fully, to feel it viscerally, to open ourselves to it completely is something that many of us cannot accomplish. We may see, but it is only out of the corners of our eyes. Joanna believes that our despair keeps us from being able to see. Through our inability to be present to the depths of our own grief and fear, we shut our eyes to the world. She says that before we can fully move into empowerment we have to become people capable of moving through our grief and our tears. This is more than we thought would be asked of us, but we must have the strength to grieve. Prophetic witness moves this way.

In *The Life of the Mind*, Hannah Arendt writes about her effort to understand how Nazism succeeded in Germany. She attended the Eichmann trials in Jerusalem, and after watching witness after witness narrate the part they played in the death camps, she came to the conclusion that the explanation for atrocities was not some profound malevolence; it was a lack of thinking. Those who built and operated the death chambers, those who gave the orders and carried them out, shared a common characteristic, a kind of flatness or banality. People blandly reported turning on the gas as if they had no feeling—even in retrospect—for what this activity meant. It was as if these human beings had lost the ability to connect their actions to consequences. Arendt calls this numbness "not-thinking."

To think is to be able to see the relationships among things: the relationships between cause and effect, between one human being and another, between human beings and the earth. The prophet is one who thinks and, therefore, sees clearly the relationships among things.

We especially need to recover from numbness and thoughtlessness to deal with racism. Baldwin's point, in part, is that racism in America has flourished because of white people's blindness toward its complex structural embodiments. An example from the recent history of Unitarian Universalism illustrates this point. At the 1993 General Assembly in Charlotte, North Carolina, the Thomas Jefferson District hosted the Thomas Jefferson Ball, inviting people to come dressed in period costumes. African Americans asked, "Shall we come wearing chains?" Whites found themselves asking, "How could we have been so unthinking? How did we fail to remember that Jefferson owned slaves?"

Whatever the force is that causes numbness and denial, prophetic witness is the contrary force: It breaks silence, it is not content with forgetting, it faces history honestly, and then it acts in light of that knowledge. Baldwin writes in *Notes of a Native Son*,

> Neither whites nor blacks, for excellent reasons of their own, have the faintest desire to look back; but I think that the past is all that makes the present coherent, and further, that the past will remain horrible for exactly as long as we refuse to assess it honestly.

The honest assessment of the past involves not forgetting the history of slavery and not denying the fact that all of us are implicated in its history. There is not one among us who is white who has not received the inheritance of white privilege. We do not turn that fact around by disassociating ourselves from slaveholders. In fact, disassociating ourselves can leave us with the illusion that we have accomplished something, when all we have done is tried to shore up our identity as pure people, untainted by sin. I am learning to see that, as a white person, my preoccupation with my innocence and perfection is the force that leads me to constantly forget, ignore, or separate myself from the realities of racism. I do not want to get my hands dirty. I want to be pure; the pursuit of purity is the heart of white supremacy. We achieve our purity by disconnecting from those we consider unacceptable.

More recently, the Thomas Jefferson District has considered abandoning Jefferson's name. This raises the question: If we renounce the name of Thomas Jefferson, how will this act be distinguished from the standard pattern of white supremacy, which seeks to purify its community of its association with the unclean? How will Unitarian Universalists maintain a commitment to face history honestly and create justice in the present? Will we just wash our hands of one great man's sins in order to redeem and distance ourselves from our own?

Prophetic witness keeps our consciousness alert to the realities of history and to the present consequences of that history. It asks us to redeem that history not by washing our hands of it but by searching for a quality of life together in which no one flourishes because of the suffering of another. It asks us to roll up our sleeves and work for racial justice. The more deeply we undertake this task, the more we will be blessed by this work.

There is a second religious task that I believe is asked of us in these difficult times: the preservation of endangered knowledge. We are living in an age when our daily life is dominated by marketplace values that belittle our humanity. The marketplace says that all we are is self-interested individuals with an insatiable need for goods. Business is conducted to maximize profits at almost any cost. For many of us, the marketplace becomes the consuming machine in which our lives are enmeshed. We lose sight of other dimensions of being human. We lose our awareness that we have intimate and meaningful relationships with one another, that we are connected to and dependent upon the earth, that we have interests that transcend our own personal lives. None of these dimensions of what it is to be human is factored into the values of the marketplace.

Perhaps those who are retired have a sense of distance from all of this, but where I live, people constantly say that their lives are overwhelmingly busy. We can do business twenty-four hours a day. We can go shopping any time we want. We can spend all of our time participating in the rhythms, patterns, and energies of the marketplace, which tells us that we are empty, needy people who can only find happiness by acquiring the wealth we need to consume products that didn't exist yesterday and that we didn't know we needed. Supposedly, in this relentless pursuit of self-interest, we will find the meaning of life.

Almost all of us know that the meaning of life cannot be attained in this narrow and manic way, but it is very hard for us to turn away from it. Theologian John Cobb says that in the mature years of his career he is putting all of his energy into analyzing and critiquing the operating assumptions of global capitalism. The reason he is doing this is that he now believes that our current economic system is the dominant religion of the world.

This observation is important. Those of us on the Left often find ourselves thinking that the religious Right is the great religious force we need to resist and engage with critically. But the religious and political Rights are handmaidens to global capitalism. This is the operational belief system that needs to be analyzed as the source of the breakdown of our relationships with each other and our relationships with the earth. After all, the primary motivation for slavery was not prejudice; it was economic advantage. Global capitalism is an inadequate religious system whose power in our lives must be dismantled. Without its conversion and transformation, without finding its right size in our lives as a whole, this dominant religious system will continue to imperil our relationships with each other and endanger the earth.

What is asked of us religiously is the capacity to preserve and access knowledge that is outside of what the dominant economic system tells us about who we are. I recommend two spiritual practices as pathways to doing this: keeping the Sabbath and tithing. These practices are extremely simple, yet they ask a great deal of us.

Keeping the Sabbath means that once every seven days—not once every seven years and not only when you're given a few vacation days, but once every seven days, you stop participating in the rat race. You choose one day out of seven not to go shopping. Not to go to work. Not to bring any work home. Instead, you give yourself and others the space to feel what it is hard to feel when you spend all your time, as Wordsworth says, "getting and spending and laying waste your powers." You give yourself time to walk in the woods, to see how the leaves of the willows are coming out and the tulips are bending in the wind. You give yourself time to sit at the table with friends, to welcome the friendless, and to talk with one another. You give yourself time to read, think, and reflect. You take the time to face the realities of injustice and suffering in the world and to grieve the losses and the legacies of violence that mark our lives. You set aside time to gather with the religious community to pray, give thanks, and hear the wisdom of the ages. You stop the madness and rest. You open yourself to the beauty and meaning of life, to all those tender capacities within yourself and all those dear relationships with others that you cherish. You find a way to know all of these things that the marketplace can neither give nor take away.

To keep the Sabbath is a radical act of resistance to a culture that has lost track of the meaning of life. A day of rest helps us become capable of entering into profound and sustained engagement with a culture that needs our creative witness and our work for change.

Tithing is just as simple as keeping the Sabbath, just as ancient in its wisdom, and even more unfamiliar to Unitarian Universalists. I do not mean tithing in spirit, in principle, or as a metaphor. I mean giving away ten percent of your income. The way I was taught to do this is to give ten percent before taxes. I count myself lucky to have been taught to tithe as a child. It is a fundamental spiritual practice that liberal religious people would be wise to follow.

Tithing can be learned. In fact, I don't think that anyone who tithes has come to it by any way other than being taught. In third grade, I was taught by my parents, when they gave me my first allowance of fifty cents. They explained to me that ten percent of fifty cents was five cents, and they gave me a pledge card to the church and an envelope. My first tithe was five cents a week to the church.

One reason tithing is important is that causes we believe in will flourish if we share more of our resources. We need to open our eyes to the fact that the religious Right has gained influence through the help of conservative Christians who tithe. If we want our values to shape our society, we need to generously fund organizations that support them. But there is a deeper, more fundamental spiritual reason to tithe. I realized it listening to a member of the first congregation I served. It was pledge drive Sunday, and people had been asked to talk about why they give to the church.

One congregation member stood up and said, "I first began to tithe because I was taught to do so by my church and my church taught me to obey its teachings. I tithed because I saw obedience as the heart of faithfulness. But as I matured in my faith, I began to understand that obedience was not all that important and could even be destructive. I continued to tithe, however, because a different reason had come to me. I tithed because the people I most loved and admired tithed: my parents and leaders of the religious community whose lives really challenged me by their goodness. I wanted to be like them so I tithed in imitation of those that I loved."

He went on, "But as my faith matured further, I came to my own reason for tithing. This is why I do it now: I do it because to tithe is to tell the truth about who I am. If I did not tithe, it would say that I was a person who had nothing to give, a person who had received nothing from life. A person who did not matter to the larger society or whose life's meaning was in providing for his own needs alone. But in fact, who I am is the opposite of all of these things. I am a person who has something to give. I am a person who has received abundantly from life. I am a person whose presence matters in the world, and I am a person whose life has meaning because I am connected to and care about many things larger than myself. If I did not tithe, I would lose track of these truths about who I am."

The endangered knowledge—the knowledge that we are at risk of forgetting or even never coming to deeply know—is that to be a human being is to live in a world that has richly provided for us, a world that we are to steward. We must not lose track of the knowledge that we inhabit a world that has enough land to feed all of Earth's people and enough resources to shelter all of Earth's children. We must preserve awareness that our presence matters, or we fail to act as people who are a blessing to life. We will become people who tear the fabric of life. The fullness of who we are as human beings is endangered knowledge in our culture. We need religious practices like Sabbath keeping and tithing to teach us a different sense of ourselves and the world. Learning to endure the shamanistic journey is our other great religious task.

In a shamanistic journey, one moves into the places of grief, pain, loss, and breakdown; faces squarely the losses we have suffered and the dangers we face; and discovers afresh the capacity to feel, one's longings and passion for life, and one's vision for what can be. The shamanistic journey brings about the kind of transformation in which we let go of what has been and enter into a place of new knowledge and new vision.

Like the Sabbath and tithing, the shamanistic journey has to be learned. One way that we learn it is by participation in religious communities that symbolically reenact such journeys. This speaks to the importance of ritual in our lives. By allowing us to symbolically move through them, rituals teach our souls the passages that we will be required to endure in our living.

For example, the Passover story in the Jewish tradition is a form of shamanistic journey. It marks the journey from an established world that was unjust, through a wilderness of confusion, fear, and hunger, and into a place of revelation, of new ways of living. After the terror and glory of Mt. Sinai, the squabbling conflicts, the long desert journey, and the river crossing, the people of Israel finally enter a new land. Passover ritualizes a collective shamanistic journey.

Each year, the Christian tradition recalls a shamanistic journey in the death and resurrection of Jesus. The rituals of Lent and Holy Week reenact the capacity of human beings to extinguish the presence of the sacred in the world, to break ties with one another and flee from the best that is asked of us. Easter recalls people to the abiding presence of grace and creativity that draws us to each other, to the earth, and to holiness itself. It promises us that there is life beyond the ways we violate and destroy the gifts of life.

There are many expressions of the shamanistic journey, including those narrated in Native American myths and rituals. As Unitarian Universalists, we are willing to open ourselves to wisdom from many sources, but it is this particular kind of wisdom to which we especially need to pay attention now. We need to pay attention not only by rehearsing the stories but by allowing ourselves to enter into the experiences. This means a worship life that moves beyond our heads and into our hearts and bodies. In such a worship life, we can begin to learn what we must do in the rest of our lives.

The shamanistic journey is important because we are living in a culture that must be transformed. The many systems of injustice and oppression that pattern our lives are not adequate. We are capable of creating a more just, abundant, and sustainable life for ourselves and for all of the earth's people. We must offer religious leadership to a society that is called to change its fundamental ways of being. We must become people who personally know the pathway of conversion and can bear witness to this conversion in a culture that will do everything it can to resist change. We must offer leadership so that the larger society can be converted.

We must also recognize those in our midst who carry the shaman's wisdom. If we pay attention, we will see that they are found among those who are targeted as dangerous to the dominant culture. Those who understand the shamanistic journey are found in the black church; they are found among lesbian, gay, bisexual, and transgender people; they are found among women artists, and people of persecuted faiths and outcast cultures. Those most at risk in the dominant culture have been rightly named as the most dangerous to that culture because they know a way through transformation. At present, the dominant culture is resisting the changes that must come if we are to be a world in which "the least of these" survive. Our responsibility as a religious community includes offering sanctuary and shelter to the religious visionaries, the people of soul who know the way ahead. We have performed this service before. Sometimes we, ourselves, have been such witnesses. Even when we cannot do it ourselves, we are capable of recognizing the saints, the sages, the great souls among us. We can support and defend them and heed their teachings.

The story of Moses illustrates what it means to see the beauty and glory of life. Moses was out in the pasture when suddenly he saw a bush on fire. He heard a voice from the bush say, "Now you must go back to Egypt where I have seen my people in their travail. You must lead them to freedom." And Moses, of course, said what any sane person would say: "Ask someone else to do this!" The voice was insistent: "No, you must go and offer this leadership." But Moses wrangled with God and said, "No, my brother Aaron would be much better." We ourselves sometimes say, "The Quakers would be much better. The progressive Catholics would be much better. The Reconstructionist Jews, they could do this!" But the voice is insistent, "No, you must go. You must do this."

Many of us have seen the bush on fire, too—in the dawn light that skims over the treetops of the cedars, in the face of a newborn child, or in the middle of a church service when people were singing. We have asked the question, "What shall we do with all this beauty?" I believe that beauty confronts us with the requirement that we place ourselves among the saviors, the redeemers, the leaders in the protection of life. The ancient story tells us that once you have seen the bush on fire—once you have seen the beauty—you only have two choices: You either have to close your eyes to the beauty or you have to go back to Egypt and set the people free.

More is asked of us than we could have imagined. The beauty of life is such that it will not let us go until we have offered the blessing we have to give. So let the beauty we have seen become the good that we do, and let us not wrest ourselves free from the claim that life places upon us until we, in faith with all those who have gone before us, place ourselves among those who bless the world.

SOUL MUSIC

MUSIC SOUNDS IN THE DEPTHS OF OUR HEARTS. It is music of joy: voices in the coffee shop, a clattering ragtime, or the wind whooshing through the sea grasses, a graceful waltz. It is music of sadness: the cello, a cinnamon sound soft and low through the broken windows of Sarajevo, the bagpipe keening plaintively as a community gathers to mourn its dead. It is music of assurance: a mother singing, "Sleep my child. Let peace attend thee, all through the night," or the congregation, "Amazing Grace, how sweet the sound." This music that sounds in the depths of our hearts is soul.

To live with soul is to live deeply rooted in knowing and feeling that we are connected to one another and to the earth, that our life is held in the embrace of something larger than ourselves—a wisdom, a presence, a grace "whose beatitude is accessible to us," says Ralph Waldo Emerson in his essay "The Over-Soul." To have soul is to hear life's deep music and to move in response to its pulse, rhythm, and harmony. To have soul is to be awake to life. To have soul is to live with a sensitive awareness of the real presence of other human beings and the earth. It is turning your hands to the work of justice and compassion, your mind to the call of wisdom, your heart to decisions for life. It is making your whole being an act of praise.

On this small planet adrift in the ocean of stars, we feel the pull of our ties to one another, the pulse of the earth held close to our ear, the rocking of our being in the bosom of Abraham. This is the music of soul.

But we can lose the ability to hear this music. In *Pornography and Silence*, Susan Griffin writes, "We never lose soul but we lose knowledge of soul. We cease to know ourselves . . . and others. We begin to believe the world is soulless, and our belief makes this true." When we become deaf to one another's presence and relate violently to each other, we lose the music. Our personal soul as well as the soul of our nation and of our global community rests in our ability to honor the relational bonds of life.

The breaking of these bonds silences the music. The violence of September 11 shattered the bonds of the human community. The daily news of suicide bombers and tank assaults in Israel and Palestine and the ongoing aggression in Iraq and Afghanistan leave our souls numb with grief, shock, and anger.

Our souls are weary. Even before the anguishing events of the dawn of the twenty-first century, there was much in the news to trouble our souls: the increasing criminalization of the poor, hate crimes, exploitation of the earth's natural resources, widening gaps between the rich and the poor on a global scale, resurgent racism, neglect of children, gunshots in school libraries. These painful realities suggest that as a society—as a world—we are not moving to the rhythm of soul and its tender imperative that we love one another.

The poet Adrienne Rich says losing track of the music of soul is like being a child torn from your mother. She writes,

> At most we're allowed a few months
> of simply listening to the simple line
> of a woman's voice singing a child
> against her heart. Everything else is too soon,
> too sudden, the wrenching-apart, that woman's heartbeat
> heard ever after from a distance,
> the loss of that ground-note echoing
> whenever we are happy, or in despair.

To be estranged from soul is to be in a state of anesthetized feeling. Political philosopher Hannah Arendt said that Adolf Eichmann's monstrous evil as an engineer of the Holocaust was not the result of malevolence but of a banal thoughtlessness, a loss of awareness of any real connection between himself, his actions, and other human beings. Alfred North Whitehead defines anesthetization as "the slow paralysis of surprise" and calls it evil's most dangerous form.

Estranged from soul, we are numb—not fully awake to life, to feeling, to seeing and knowing the world or to taking part in it in a soulful way. In the state of anesthetized feeling we risk doing harm to one another. Cut off from the music that sounds in the depth of our hearts, we may turn aside from those who are suffering or we may overlook the breathtakingly beautiful. As author Alice Walker puts it, we may walk by the color purple and not even notice. This, she says, angers God. Estranged from soul we neither laugh nor cry, we neither savor nor save the world.

If we are to move in the world as agents of grace, not engineers of evil, as active contributors to the structures that uphold life, not anesthetized accomplices in systems that harm life, then our souls need to be awake. This means we have to pay attention to the ways that our own souls have been numbed by our experiences. Some of us live haunted by the violence that has touched our lives. Some of us struggle with rejection and exclusion. Some of us bear a protracted grief that leaves us numb to feeling. Some of us work hard, our days filled with tasks and responsibilities, but when we pause to catch our breath we are frightened by a sense of emptiness. However it happens, many of us are not strangers to the experience of losing our soulfulness. We move through our days in a cloud of numbness, aware that we aren't fully feeling or thinking. We become passive, living with a sense that we are powerless in the presence of overwhelming systems of violence.

When our own soulfulness is lost to us, we need experiences of transforming grace that awaken the music in the depths of our hearts, reconnect us to our power to make a difference in the world, and renew our capacity to think and to feel. Such reawakening is possible. Even those who are physically deaf can feel the vibration and rhythm of music. I have seen the deaf dance. Human beings can be restored to the music of life.

At the end of World War II, Lyle Grunkenmeir came home to Iowa. His mother and sister waited for his return. The day he came home—the only veteran to return alive to that town— everyone came out to meet him. As the train pulled into the station, the band played and the mayor was there to shake his hand.

But as his sister later told me that the man who climbed off the train was not the lively, cheerful boy who had left for war. He was a ghost. He didn't seem to recognize anyone, not his mother, sister, or friends. In response to the crowd's rousing welcome, he stared mutely. Blank.

His family took him home to the farm, where he sat in the old rocking chair in the parlor. He did not speak or move and would barely eat. He continued in this state for days that spilled into weeks that flowed into months. No one in this town knew about posttraumatic shock; they only knew that Lyle's soul was lost somewhere.

Lyle's sister, Maxine, decided to stay by him. Whenever she could, she would come and sit with him, and she would talk. She'd tell him about the church potluck: who was there, what they ate, what each young woman wore. She'd tell him about the conversation she'd overheard at the store in town, and how high the crops had grown. She told him how the wind that day had blown the clean laundry into the tomatoes. When she ran out of things to say, she would just sit with him, snapping beans, mending socks. And he sat there, silent, like a stone. Rocking.

One night, while Maxine was knitting quietly beside him, Lyle's eyes filled with tears. The tears spilled over and ran down his frozen face. Maxine went to her brother and put her arms around him. Held in his sister's embrace, he began to cry full force, great sobs of anguish bursting from deep inside him.

Then he began to talk, and he would not stop. He talked of the cold, the fear, the noise, the death of his buddies, the long marches, and then the human beings in the camps, the mass graves, the smell. He talked all night until the dawn light began to creep across the fields. Maxine listened to everything Lyle had to say. Then she went into the kitchen, and she cooked him breakfast. They ate together, and then Lyle went out and did the morning chores.

The poet Kabir writes, "The flute of interior time is played whether we hear it or not. What we mean by 'love' is its sound coming in."

This is how soul comes back to us: One human being stays with another human being until the numbed person is able to speak of silenced experiences. The healing comes as the story is spoken by one and witnessed by another who is able to be present to the depth of pain without running away. Then the lost soul returns to flesh, to communion, to the world of sense and conversation and ordinary work. We can do this for one another, be present in a way that calls forth the return of soul. The love that saves our souls is expressed by staying with the heavy work of tending to buried pain. It also can be expressed in acts of grace that have a surprising simplicity and lightness.

In Seattle in the early 1980s, I served the Wallingford United Methodist church at a time when antigay sentiment was heating up in our city. Our denomination had just banned the ordination of lesbian and gay people, and the congregation decided to take a proactive stand in supporting them.

We wanted to express hospitality and welcome, but we quickly discovered that those who had been kicked out of church weren't going to return just because we hung out a welcome sign. There was no basis for trust that we meant what we said. How did people know that we weren't trying to lure them into the church so we could then convict them of their sin?

No one just came to church. They called first. Testing the waters, they asked, "Is this the church that says lesbian and gay people are welcome?" At first, we did not always know if the caller was a person looking for a church that was genuinely welcoming or someone who felt our stand was wrong and wanted to make sure we knew exactly where hell was and how close we were to falling in. Nina, our church administrator became highly adept at handling these calls. In response to the opening question, she would carefully explain our church's stand: We accepted people of diverse sexual orientations, we welcomed people as they were, and the fellowship of our church and its activities was fully open to all.

She told me that, eventually, every caller would come around to saying, "The real reason I'm calling is. . . ." One day, the caller said, "The real reason I'm calling is that I am a man, but I like to dress up in women's clothes. What I want to know is, if I come to church in a dress, will I be welcome?"

Nina pondered for a second and said, "Is it a really ugly dress?"

The next Sunday, the caller did come to church wearing a lovely red Chanel suit, complete with hat and gloves. She was warmly welcomed.

Soul comes back to us in tears that break through silence and in great laughter that shakes the foundations of this world's structures of denial and exclusion. The church must be such a place of tears and laughter that welcomes the truth of our pain and accepts us in all our humanity. A religious community in which these things can happen is a sanctuary for the recovery of soul and a school for the transformation of society. This is why we need the liberal church. This is why the work of progressive religious communities is so important.

Our mission is to enable the recovery of soul. We accomplish it as we bring our humanity to one another, as Maxine did for Lyle, and as we offer our gracious hospitality where the dominant society closes the door, as Nina and the Wallingford United Methodist Church did. A religious community in which these things can happen enables people to develop the depth and courage needed to stand for the goodness of human life and the beauty of the earth and against those acts that humiliate, punish, or divide us or denigrate the ecology of the planet.

Now more than ever, we must be dedicated to soulful living, to participating in the world in a soulful way. We must cherish our congregations as places where we can come together to welcome one another's tears and laughter and to think deeply about the things that matter most. We must continue to be advocates in our society for a way of being together in which the bonds of connection that weave us together in one life are honored, not broken.

Let us make it our aim to move in harmony with the deep music that is always sounding. Even when we have momentarily lost our ability to hear or feel it, the music is there. Let us respond to the rhythm and harmony that pulses through life, ever refreshing our souls. And let us move in the world as singers and dancers of the spirit, composers of justice, and artists of peace.

LOVE FIRST

DURING THE CIVIL WAR, Unitarian minister Thomas Starr King worked tirelessly for abolition. A mere five feet tall, he said, "I may be small, but when I am mad I weigh a ton." Like Starr King, we live in a nation that is at war and that has lost its way, a nation in which our presence as progressive people of faith is needed and even our anger is required. Starr King insisted that the pulpit should be used to address national issues because our religious and ethical values are not simply personal, they are about how we relate to one another and to the earth. King said, "We are not intended to be separate, private persons, but rather fibers, fingers and limbs. . . . There can be no such thing as justice until men in large masses are rightly related to each other."

Starr King's anger held the weight of burning love. His ministry was fired by passionate caring that could not tolerate seeing life needlessly harmed by stupidity, lack of attention, inadequate organization, or narrow self-interest by people in power.

Many of us were outraged by the aftermath of Hurricane Katrina. Scenes of people swept away by flood waters, crowding into inadequate shelters, desperately waving homemade signs from rooftops that said "Help Us!" and hoping the helicopters overhead would not fly away. Many waited for days in sweltering heat for food and water. More than thirteen hundred people died. These events, combined with our government's neglectful response, revealed how deeply our nation is off course. We didn't simply witness a natural disaster. What unfolded before our eyes was the cumulative effect of our nation's decisions about how we relate to the environment, how we manage the production and distribution of wealth, how white privilege plays itself out, how we approach security, and how we relate to knowledge and information. All of these topics are religious issues on which the leadership of progressive people of faith is needed.

Even conservatives raised the alarm. Paul Craig Roberts, a former editor and columnist for the *Wall Street Journal* and now a senior research fellow at the Hoover Institute at Stanford, writes,

> The U. S. has lost its largest and most strategic port, thousands of lives, and 80% of one of America's most historic cities is under water. If terrorists had achieved this result, it would rank as the greatest terrorist success in history. . . . Every expert and newspapers as distant as Texas saw the New Orleans catastrophe coming. But President Bush and his insane government preferred war in Iraq to protecting Americans at home. Bush's war left the Corps of Engineers only 20% of the funding to protect New Orleans from flooding. . . . Not content with leaving New Orleans unprotected, it took the Bush administration *five days* to get the remnants of the National Guard not serving in Iraq, along with desperately needed food and water, to devastated New Orleans. . . . Bush has squandered the lives and health of thousands of people. He has run through hundreds of billions of borrowed dollars. He has lost America's reputation and its allies. With barbaric torture and destruction of our civil liberty, he has stripped America of its inherent goodness and morality. . . . What will it take for Americans to reestablish accountability in their government? . . . What disaster will next spring from Bush's incompetence?

Roberts calls this incompetence and makes Bush the target of his rage, but our analysis must be broader. It is not one heedless human being with too much power who put us where we are, and the course of our nation will not be altered in the direction of justice and compassion by removing one president from office.

What we need is a revolution in our values, a revolution that turns our attention more reverently and responsibly to the interdependent, relational character of life. What we need is a spiritual and practical revolution that embodies love for neighbor and for the world through sustaining structures of care and responsibility.

Five days after the hurricane, President Bush toured some of the devastation in Louisiana, Alabama, and Mississippi and said this was a time for people to love their neighbors as themselves. His comment suggests a view of love as a gesture of kindly help when the situation has become horrendously dire.

Such a view of love is not sufficient.

Loving our neighbor implicates us in loving the whole network of life. Science has given us photographs of the earth from space. We can see we are one blue globe, wreathed with clouds. We know the crust of the earth floats on a core of fire. Even the rocks are part of a complex flow of elements that fold down into that molten core and rise again. We dwell in our cities and towns on a living, breathing planet molded by transforming fire, flowing waters, the exhalations of trees, and the inbreathing of animals. This interconnectedness of all things calls for wisdom and reverence. We cannot trample this landscape of life as ignorant fools and expect to be safe. We cannot turn from our bonds and obligations for and with one another and expect everyone to be okay. We cannot love after the fact and expect love to be able to save life. Maybe in the end love will save us all, but it has a lot better chance at the beginning.

We need to love from the start—not as an emergency strategy when everything has gone wrong. We need to love our neighbors as ourselves through economic systems that pay a living wage for labor instead of indulging in policies that allow the rich to get richer and the poor to be left behind when the storm comes. We need to love the world through reverence that fosters observant attention to the intricate relationality of life. It is not sufficient to relegate love to a few moments of sentiment or to celebrate it in effusive accolades about the compassion of the American people. It is not sufficient to expect love to be the domestic help that will wipe the tears from the eyes of the children living in the house of a cruel master. It is not enough to address injustice in the moment. The whole pathway—the whole road from Jerusalem to Jericho, as Martin Luther King Jr. said in a 1968 speech—must be just. If we can learn to love first, not last, then love may save us.

Rev. Joseph Lowery, one of our nation's great civil rights leaders, was interviewed on CNN in the storm's aftermath. The young announcer asked the old activist, "Do you think the tragedy we are seeing in New Orleans is the result of racism?" Lowery paused for a moment. "You cannot reduce an event of this complexity to one thing," he answered. "Part of the problem is just plain incompetence. But yes, of course, what we are seeing is racism. It is also classism and environmental irresponsibility. We cannot go on treating each other and the earth this way. We must learn again to live with reverence."

We must learn again to live with reverence. Reverence is a form of love. It is a response to life that falls on its knees before the rising sun and bows down before the mountains. It puts its palms together in the presence of the night sky and the myriad galaxies and recognizes, as poet Langston Hughes tells us, "beautiful are the stars, beautiful too are the faces of my people." Reverence greets all humanity as sacred. It genuflects before the splendor of the grass and the magnificence of the trees. It respects the complexity, the beauty, and the magnitude of creation and does not presume to undo its intricate miracles. Instead, it gives life reverent attention, seeking to know, understand, and cooperate with life's ways.

Reverence for life has to be learned. It is not just a feeling; it is a way of life that is manifested in more than an isolated moment of appreciation for nature or awe before its destructive or creative power. Reverence involves full-fledged devotion enacted in deeds of care and responsibility. It involves knowledge, study, and attention.

Our society is currently guided by a worldview that is insufficiently grounded in reverence. Religiously, it is a worldview that regards the earth itself as trash—a planet that God is soon going to discard in a plan to wipe this world away and create a new one. Economically, the dominant worldview regards human beings as self-interested individuals, motivated only by their personal desire to consume. And scientifically, it sees existence as devoid of value, atomistic, disconnected, and mechanistic. Such inadequate views are tearing our world to tatters by lack of regard for the communal character of life.

Holy regard for knowledge is at the heart of our religious faith. A few years ago, when I visited my congregation's partner church in Okland, Transylvania, Rev. Levente Keleman took me into the sanctuary to see the ceiling of the four-hundred-year-old Unitarian church in his village. In typical Transylvanian style, the church has a wooden ceiling, crisscrossed with beams creating a lattice of deep squares, which are painted with folk art depicting flowers and plants. Near the center of the sanctuary, the ceiling harbors a surprising image, a golden sun surrounded by circling planets in a star-spangled indigo sky. It is a diagram of the Copernican solar system. At a time when religion was opposing science, our ancestors in the remote mountains and valleys of Transylvania built sanctuaries that affirmed the discoveries of science. They did so even when the dominant religious culture advocated ideologies that allowed no new revelation and insisted that the old theories of how the world came to be had to be taught in the public schools.

Holy regard matters now more than ever. In 1514, when Copernicus reimagined the nature of the solar system, it was the result of a lifetime of careful study. One of his students described his method. In his *First Report*, Rheticus writes about Copernicus's way of working:

> My teacher always had before his eyes the observations of all ages together with his own, assembled in order as in catalogues; then when some conclusion must be drawn or contribution made to the science and its principles, he proceeds from the earliest observations to his own, seeking the mutual relationship which harmonizes them all; the results thus obtained by correct inference under the guidance of Urania he then compares with the hypothesis of Ptolemy and the ancients; and having made a most careful examination of these hypotheses, he finds that astronomical proof requires their rejection; he assumes new hypotheses, not indeed without divine inspiration and the favour of the gods; by applying mathematics, he geometrically establishes the conclusions which can be drawn from them by correct inference; he then harmonizes the ancient observations and his own with the hypotheses which he has adopted; and after performing all these operations he finally writes down the laws of astronomy.

This is the kind of intelligent, persistent care that enables revolutionary new understanding, and it is the lack of this kind of love that is harming our nation now. But the presence of such studious and grounded care can transform the world.

Our task now is to do what we can to advance reverence for life and deepen the promise of love. Let us dedicate ourselves to the thinking, researching, practice, and learning that will bring more love into the world. Let us be witnesses for the new science that tells us how connected all life is and let us work for social policies that embody our responsibility for one another and for the earth. Let us give reverent attention in our worship life and our educational work to serving the beauty and goodness of life. Let us be a shelter for truths that the dominant culture would rule out. Let us make love the first—not the last—resort.

This is an audacious task for a small movement of progressive people of faith but to paraphrase Thomas Starr King, we may be small, but when we are mad we weigh a ton. The weight of our passionate caring can help turn the world around.

Choose to Bless the World

I first met the process theologian Charles Hartshorne when I was a graduate student at the Claremont School of Theology. I was assigned to help Charles's wife, Dorothy, catalogue his papers. Each spring break, I would travel to the Hartshornes' home to spend some time working with Dorothy and Charles. This was my introduction to their world and way of life, and it was an important part of my education in process thought.

One afternoon, Charles and I took a break from our cataloging to go bird watching. That is when I discovered that Charles did not drive. Thinking of my own grandfather who was deeply distressed when his failing reflexes resulted in the loss of his driver's license, I sympathetically asked the eighty-year-old Charles, "When did you have to give up driving?" He paused to think for a minute and, completing his mental calculations, said, "I'd say about forty-three years ago." He saw my surprise and explained, "I could see the environmental damage that would result from too many automobiles and resolved to use public transportation or walk."

Years later I was at an academic conference in which process thought was being roundly criticized. The enthusiastic attacker was detailing the failings of process theologians; they were heady and abstract and gave no attention to practical ethics or social justice. I asked if the critic drove a car. His argument couldn't stand up in the face of Hartshorne's relinquishment of the automobile.

While this may seem a small detail in the life of a great philosopher, the story of Charles and his automobile illustrates what I see as the gifts of process theology. Process theology helps us heal a philosophical dualism that does violence to the world, and it empowers human beings to be responsible moral agents who, with God, co-create a more just, beautiful, and sustainable world.

We live in a culture in which there is a long philosophical history that devalues the world and denies its real presence. The group suicide of the Heaven's Gate cult in San Diego is symptomatic of our culture's philosophic presuppositions. To these cult members, the body was a vehicle for a nonmaterial soul, and the death of the body was considered insignificant in the career of a soul that would travel beyond this earthly life to another world.

Though it is rarely portrayed so vividly, the philosophical view that splits mind and body, spirit and earth, into two separable realities—one valuable, the other unimportant—is pervasive in our culture. After all, what difference is there, finally, between these cult members and the Boeing computer scientists who, back when the Cold War was still cold, were working on a U. S. government contract to design a computer system that would effectively carry on a nuclear exchange with the Soviet Union, even if all the military personnel—and the rest of us along with them—were dead. We were investing money in ensuring that the United States would win a nuclear war, even if none of us was here. I understand the argument that this capability would function as a deterrent to Soviet attack. Still, the whole enterprise reflects a mindset in which the body of the earth and all its creatures is devalued to the point of insignificance. And the realm of abstract principles is served as if it had some kind of existence of greater value than life.

There is a history to this dualistic thinking. When Descartes said, "I think therefore I am," his revelation articulated an emerging worldview that, as it evolved, led to a greater and greater split between mind and matter. Since the dawn of the Enlightenment, Western philosophy has been preoccupied with its important discovery that the perceiving subject, the thinker, shapes the world by projection, perspective, and interpretation. In its emphasis on the contribution of the knower to what is known, the Enlightenment has led to several centuries of critical examination of the prejudice and perspective brought to the world by each person as an interpreter of the world. Postmodernity or, as some view it, hypermodernity takes the Enlightenment emphasis on the interpreter to its extreme. For example, postmodern literary criticism focuses on the reader of texts and argues that, finally, there are no texts, only readings of texts.

In this philosophical development the world itself—that which is tasted, touched, felt, seen, and heard, that which is *other* than the perceiver—has become distant, devalued, and nearly invisible. The concept that beauty is in the eye of the beholder captures the result of the dominant Western worldview. It is a remarkable statement. Beauty is not in the rose. The rose does not contribute quality, character, or value to the one who encounters it. Beauty is the construct, the projection, the value placed upon the rose by the one who sees, touches, or smells. In this mindset, the rose itself is devoid of intrinsic value and, by extension, so is the world. Creation is valueless, a blank screen onto which the perceiver projects value.

It is not a far step from there to the point at which the world disappears altogether. This is the problem of philosophical solipsism: the confidence that I exist accompanied by the profound doubt that anything outside of me exists. How do I know it is not all a dream? The poet Matthew Arnold confronted this uncertainty and the resulting despair in the nineteenth century in his poem "Dover Beach":

> The world, which seems to lie before us like a land of
>   dreams,
> so various, so beautiful, so new,
> hath really neither joy, nor love, nor light,
> nor certitude, nor peace, nor help for pain,

and we are here, as on a darkling plain,
swept with confused alarms of struggle and flight
where ignorant armies clash by night.

To ignore the world as an actual place is to imagine it empty of value, except for that which we bestow upon it. As the world recedes into obscurity, only the subject is bathed in the light of reality. This is the legacy of the Enlightenment. While it gave us the important gift of self-critical awareness, the Enlightenment also contributed to a construction of the self as master of the world. The knower paints meaning and value onto the world. The knower is active, even aggressive; the world is passive, a blank canvas.

This is not just a lesson in the history of ideas; it is a description of how we actually behave. In our debates over how to manage old-growth forests, we discuss the different values the forest has to competing subjects and interests, but we do not ascribe to the forest any intrinsic value, power, or presence. Once the earth has disappeared from our minds, its relentless exploitation is easy and its careful stewardship difficult. We can be comfortable consuming its resources because we are the bestowers of value; the resources themselves are without meaning. We matter. Earth doesn't.

This mindset is implicated not only in violence against the earth but in other forms of violence, too. The general public was charmed by the movie celebrating *Penthouse* publisher Larry Flynt. Flynt is a philosopher of the old school that separates spirit and flesh and then associates maleness with spirit and femaleness with flesh. The most memorable and brutal image on the cover of Flynt's magazine is of a woman being fed into a grinder and turned into "fresh meat." Woman becomes material to be possessed and treated in whatever way the possessor pleases; she has no value of herself. Feminist Susan Griffin calls this worldview the pornographic mind. It is a mind that does not know itself to be intimately implicated in a body and that imagines itself to be separated from the world. It is an alienated mindset that allows and commits violence.

We can also see these alienating dichotomies at work in racial categorization and oppression. In a cartoon that shows a crowd of people of many different colors, one white person is shown with a bubble of thought: "Gee, what if I am not the main character in this story?" Womanist theologian Delores Williams calls this "white narcissism," the habit of whites to think that it's all about us, that we are the main characters in a story in which our freedom from guilt, our desire for innocence, and our need to be well regarded are the main plot lines. So great is our narcissism that whites often miss the point that, in dynamics of racial categorization and oppression, there are other people in the story, and that the story is about them too and about our relationships together. The ability to see the other as having intrinsic value and to act in accordance with that knowledge is an ability that we who are white need in order to be allies with people of color in building more just systems and loving relationships.

But our inherited worldview makes it harder for us to see intrinsic value in that which is other than ourselves. It is no accident that the dawn of the Enlightenment coincided with the beginning of racial categorization by white European intellectuals at the University of Heidelberg. Their belief in superior and inferior races—some closer to the spirit and some more animal and material—justified the colonial exploitation of African peoples and the displacement and colonization of Native Americans on this continent.

The philosophical hubris of the Enlightenment undergirds racism, sexism, and the exploitation of the earth. To act in ethically just ways requires a change of mind. It requires a philosophy of humility rather than hubris, of relationality rather than solipsism. Process thought is a philosophical system that overcomes the dualistic split that privileges mind over matter, subject over object, and knower over known.

Charles Hartshorne and Alfred North Whitehead have pursued a different course from the dominant stream of dualistic Western philosophy. Instead of splitting mind and matter, process thought reconceives matter as process, or activity. It does so partly under the influence of post-Newtonian physics, which has gone beyond the notion that the material world is built up from aggregates of tiny pieces of matter, atoms. Post-Newtonian physics does possess an atomic understanding of reality, but the atoms are not bits of matter; they are tiny events. The closer you look, the more material seems like dance patterns—waltzes and tangos of quantums and quarks.

Our old physical notion of matter is gone, and without one partner in the mind/matter dualism, the other partner can't be conceived of in the same way. In the old philosophy, mind and matter were in a codependent relationship. Each one depended on the other to play its part, but matter stopped acting like its old self. What had once appeared to be concrete material now looked more like an energy dance. Particles aren't there all the time; they blip in and out of existence. As far as present-day physics can tell, there is no such thing as hard matter that endures through time. The building blocks simply aren't blocks. Without the old material world to house it, the notion of spirit as a distinct, separate reality disappears, too. Mind or spirit cannot escape from the material world because there is no material world to escape from.

Process metaphysics conceives afresh the basic character of reality. Instead of aggregates of atoms that are bits of matter, process thought conceives of the world as aggregates of little bits of activity. Each activity is a discreet entity that becomes and passes away in the blink of an eye. Its existence is a moment of feeling. What is felt is every other entity in the universe as it flows into just that momentary point on the space-time continuum.

Picture the universe like Indra's net, an image from Hinduism. Indra's net is an interconnected web of countless strands, and at every intersection there is a jewel drop of water that reflects the whole. Process philosophy sees the universe as the plentitude of these jewel drops, each holding the whole in precisely the way the whole is reflected at that point of intersection.

Picture this bejeweled net as a spider web covered with dew. Picture the web lasting only for an instant, then disappearing, and in the next instant reappearing again, only not the same as the previous moment. It is slightly different. In each moment the whole is configured in a different way, and over time—over a series of blips—the net appears to be in motion, shimmering or undulating. These shimmers are people running, tides moving, comets soaring, grass growing, suns burning, rocks eroding. In the people running, there are emotions flowing, thoughts forming and passing, things remembered, things forgotten. And all of it is the cosmos, in an ever-changing pulsation of becoming and ceasing.

In the macrocosmic view, this becoming and ceasing universe—better called a multiverse—is comprised of a multitude of tiny jewel drops. But if we look microcosmically into each jewel drop, into what Whitehead calls an "actual occasion," we see something more: We see that the jewel drop is a moment of subjectivity, alive with feeling. The whole universe is flowing into that moment, which exists as a vessel of receptivity to all that is. This subject, in its brief moment of immediate existence, integrates the whole universe. The particular way the whole universe is held together in that moment is created by the moment itself, out of all it has felt and out of its grasp of all the possibilities of what could be.

The process view is formed to make sense of the observed and theorized phenomena of quantum mechanics and relativity theory, which suggest that each subjective moment is self-determining. This power of self-determination is a fundamental feature of reality. Reality is not, finally, caused by action, decision, will, or the influence of something outside of itself. The subject determines itself, and the observed world arises from a constant unfolding of countless individual acts of self-determination within a vast field of connection and a plentitude of possibilities. Chaos theory presents a similar understanding. It theorizes that complex, adaptive systems unfold in unpredictable ways because the system is comprised of a multitude of agents, each self-determining in response to the system as a whole.

The universe is emerging every moment, by the action of countless creators, co-creating in response to one another. The creators range in complexity and depth, from the simplest series of quarks that manifests an alternating pulse in an atomic dance, to a moment in the interstices of your brain when all the actual occasions that comprise your body spark as conscious awareness, to a moment within the fullness of the whole universe when everything is held together in such utter completeness that the moment deserves the name God.

This worldview, in which God, quarks, and a moment of your conscious awareness are all examples of the same process, variations of the same fundamental act of being/becoming, goes beyond the dualism of the Western philosophical tradition. In doing so, it opens up fresh possibilities for imagining God and our relationship to the world.

To the atheist who says, "I do not believe in God," the philosopher says, "Tell me about the God you don't believe in." The God that process theology doesn't believe in is the old God of dualistic philosophy, whose perfection is imagined as pure spirit, unsullied by the world, untouched by change, without feeling, unmoved, all-controlling, and all-knowing. The God that process theology believes in, as developed, for example, in Hartshorne's Divine Relativity, is a creator among creators, not different in kind from every other being. God is not all-knowing, because God cannot know how each moment of subjective immediacy—each dewdrop on Indra's net—will self-determine until the moment has crystallized. God is not all-powerful, because each moment is the agent of its own final crystallization.

God is supreme not in knowing everything but in receiving everything, not in controlling everything but in imagining everything. God is supreme in feeling, supreme in responsiveness. God is the subjective moment that holds the whole together with the greatest love and the cosmic embrace that tenderly welcomes all. Not the "unmoved mover" imagined by Aristotle but the being most moved by the world. Supreme in compassionate receptivity, God is also supreme in imagining what could be: an inexhaustible source of fresh possibility. Whitehead calls God "the poet of the world," whose power is like that of an artist. It is the power to inspire, persuade, and lure. In process thought, God's love is a compassionate, embracing love that receives everything. It is also an erotic, enticing love that lures. But God is not an all-determining creator. Each creature is self-creating in relationship with all other creatures, including God, so we are co-creators with the Divine. We make God, as much as God makes us.

Process thought not only conceives of God differently; it makes it possible for us to understand ourselves and the world differently. It invites us to be more responsive to the way the world is and, in this responsiveness, to surrender a way of thinking that justifies our violence. Susan Griffin articulates this other way of seeing and experiencing the world in *Woman and Nature*:

> Because we know ourselves to be made from this earth. See this grass. The patches of silver and brown. Worn by the wind. The grass reflecting all that lives in the soil. The light. The grass needing the soil. With roots deep in the earth. And patches of silver. Like the patches of silver in our hair. Worn by time. This bird flying low over the grass. Over the tules. The cattails, sedges, rushes, reeds, over the marsh. Because we know ourselves to be made from this earth. Temporary as this grass. Wet as this mud. Our cells filled with water. Like the mud of the swamp. Heather growing here because of the damp. Sphagnum moss floating on the surface, on the water standing in these pools. Places where the river washes out. Where the earth was shaped by the flow of lava. Or by the slow movements of glaciers. Because we know ourselves to be made from this earth, and shaped like the earth, by what has gone before.

When we know ourselves to be made from this earth, we do not look to life beyond the grave as a place of liberation or greater meaning. We look to this life—this world—as the locus of the sacred, and ourselves as part of it. We do not see the world as a blank screen onto which we project whatever values please us, and we do not presume that we can cut down the old-growth forest and that the only loss will be to us. We will be more likely to give up our automobiles, because the earth is not our possession to abuse and discard as we please but has value in and of itself. We understand ourselves to be part of a plenitude of being, all of which is endowed with creativity and subjectivity, each part of which is intimately connected to, influenced by, and influencing all others.

When Charles Hartshorne gave up driving his car, he was acting from a perspective of critical examination of cultural assumptions and an analysis of how these assumptions would have consequences for future generations. He acted not just for himself but also out of social concern. He acted as if he were a part of a world: a world of extended social relations, a world that had intrinsic value and not just value for him. He took an action not just because it pleased him personally but also because it made a positive contribution toward all life, not only human life but also the lives of the red-winged blackbirds and the ruby finches.

We need a revolution, a conversion. The old dominant world-view says that we are self-interested individuals, unconnected and unconcerned with one another. It says that we are the determiners of value in a world that is empty of value, apart from that which we project upon it. It says that the purpose of life is to serve ourselves and compete with our neighbors, and it adds that such competition is the given nature of things. It institutionalizes these beliefs in economic theories and systems that dominate our days.

Process thought presents another way. We are not inherently self-interested individuals. We are connected to one another, and caring for others is fundamental to our existence. To deny this is to go against the character of reality. The purpose of life is not our own well-being in isolation from all others. We are subjects, the locus of intrinsic value, but this value is always fleeting and always relational. Our well-being enters into the well-being of others, adding a measure of health or joy. Our actions matter to us and also to all the world. We live both for ourselves and for one another, in a balance that is given in the nature of things.

The purpose of life, then, is to discover the joy or well-being that simultaneously pleases us and blesses our neighbor. Every act we commit is a contribution to the world; the question is whether our actions will be a blessing or a curse. The basic question of life is not, "What do I want?" but rather, "What do I want to give?"

During those brief spring days working with Charles and Dorothy Hartshorne, I would sometimes walk with Charles from his house out to his study, a converted toolshed in the backyard. On the walk, Charles would stop every few feet, cock his head, and listen to a bird's song or watch its movement in the trees. Sometimes he would bend over to examine the buds on an azalea bush to see how soon they might be bursting forth into full flower. To him, the world was no mere screen onto which he projected his interests. The world was, and is, a real presence, full of its own value.

A few years later, on a spring evening, two of us were walking with Charles during a conference on process theology and aesthetics. We paused along the way noticing the plants, the birds, the sweet spring air. At the threshold where we would part, Charles turned around, took our hands in his, looked us squarely in the eye, and said, "Be a blessing to the world."

One is rarely given such a direct instruction, and it went straight to our hearts. When all is said and done in my life, I hope that I will have been faithful to this charge.

BENEDICTION

Your gifts
whatever you discover them to be
can be used to bless or curse the world.
The mind's power,
    The strength of the hands,
        The reaches of the heart,
the gift of speaking, listening, imagining, seeing, waiting.
Any of these can serve to feed the hungry,
    bind up wounds,
    welcome the stranger,
    praise what is sacred,
    do the work of justice
        or offer love.
Any of these can draw down the prison door
    hoard bread,
    abandon the poor,
    obscure what is holy,
    comply with injustice
        or withhold love.

You must answer this question:
What will you do with your gifts?

Choose to bless the world.

The choice to bless the world is more than an act of will
　　　a moving forward into the world
with the intention to do good.
It is an act of recognition,
　　　a confession of surprise,
　　　a grateful acknowledgment
that in the midst of a broken world
unspeakable beauty, grace and mystery abide.
There is an embrace of kindness,
that encompasses all life,
even yours.
And while there is injustice,
　　　anesthetization, or evil
there moves
a holy disturbance,
a benevolent rage,
a revolutionary love
protesting, urging, insisting
that which is sacred will not be defiled.
Those who bless the world live their life
as a gesture of thanks
for this beauty
and this rage.

The choice to bless the world
can take you into solitude
　　　to search for the sources
　　　of power and grace;
　　　native wisdom, healing, and liberation.
More, the choice will draw you into community,
　　　the endeavor shared,
　　　the heritage passed on,
　　　the companionship of struggle,

the importance of keeping faith,
the life of ritual and praise,
    the comfort of human friendship,
    the company of earth
    its chorus of life
    welcoming you.
    None of us alone can save the world.
Together—that is another possibility,
waiting.

ABOUT THE ESSAYS

THROUGH THE RUBBLE is adapted from an address delivered in April 2002 at a meeting of the Florida District of the Unitarian Universalist Association of Congregations.

AFTER THE APOCALYPSE was published in a different version in *The Transient and Permanent in Liberal Religion: Reflections from the UUMA Convocation on Ministry*, edited by Dan O'Neal, Alice Blair Wesley, and James Ishmael Ford.

NOT SOMEWHERE ELSE BUT HERE was written for a 2001 consultation on theology and racism that was convened by Unitarian Universalist Association President John Buehrens. This essay and the rest of the proceedings from that consultation were published in *Soul Work: Anti-racist Theologies in Dialogue*, edited by Marjorie Bowens-Wheatley and Nancy Palmer Jones.

YOU SHALL BE LIKE A WATERED GARDEN includes sections that appeared in a different form in the July/August 1994 issue of *The World: Selected Essays*, published by the Unitarian Universalist Ministers Association, and the Winter 1998 issue of *Open Hands*.

CORNERSTONES is adapted from a sermon preached at the rededication of the building of First Unitarian Church of San Jose, California, which had been destroyed by fire. The sermon was delivered two weeks after September 11, 2001.

HOLY WAR AND NONVIOLENT RESISTANCE is adapted from lectures delivered to the International Humanist Symposium in Boulder, Colorado, and the University Unitarian Church in Seattle, Washington. Rebecca Parker did much of the research for this chapter in preparation for a book on Christian paradise and holy war with co-author Rita Nakashima Brock, forthcoming from Beacon Press. Parts of this essay are also in *Proverbs of Ashes: Violence, Redemptive Suffering, and the Search for What Saves Us,* by Rebecca Parker and Rita Nakashima Brock.

WHAT THEY DREAMED IS OURS TO DO is based on a sermon delivered at the 1998 General Assembly of the Unitarian Universalist Association of Congregations, which appears in a different form in *Redeeming Time* by Walter Herz.

SOMETHING FAR MORE DEEPLY INTERFUSED is adapted from a sermon delivered to a group of clergy and lay people in Ohio in 1991 and published in *Thematic Preaching: An Introduction* by Jane Rzepka and Ken Sawyer.

ON THIS SHINING NIGHT is adapted from a John Murray Distinguished Lecture at the 1993 General Assembly of the Unitarian Universalist Association of Congregations, which was published in *To Bring More Light and Understanding: The John Murray Distinguished Lectures, Vol. II.*

FAMILY VALUES is based on an address delivered in response to a talk by George Lakoff, author of *Don't Think of an Elephant* and *Moral Politics* at the 2005 General Assembly of the Unitarian Universalist Association of Congregations.

WHAT SHALL WE DO WITH ALL THIS BEAUTY? is adapted from a sermon delivered in 1997 at the District Assembly of the Thomas Jefferson District of the Unitarian Universalist Association of Congregations. A version was also published in *Redeeming Time* by Walter Herz.

SOUL MUSIC has been delivered as a sermon several times between 2001 and 2004.

LOVE FIRST is based on a sermon that was first preached in the immediate aftermath of Hurricane Katrina at the Opening Convocation for the Starr King School for the Ministry.

CHOOSE TO BLESS THE WORLD is adapted from an address given at a *festschrift* for process theologian Charles Hartshorne on the occasion of his hundredth birthday in 1997.

BENEDICTION was written for the catalog of the Starr King School for the Ministry. It is inspired by Charles Hartshorne's charge, "Be a blessing to the world."

ACKNOWLEDGMENTS

We gratefully thank the communities of Starr King School for the Ministry and All Souls Church, Unitarian, in Washington, D. C., for their support, encouragement, and inspiration. We especially thank Anita Narang and Barb Greve for their assistance in preparing this manuscript for publication.